# GHOSTS and LEGENDS

ROY CHRISTIAN

DAVID and CHARLES

Newton Abbot

TO SUE

ISBN 0 7153 5703 4

Set in 11/13 point Baskerville
and printed in Great Britain
by W. J. Holman Limited Dawlish
for David & Charles (Publishers) Limited
South Devon House Newton Abbot Devon

# CONTENTS

Introduction                                        9

1  Forward from Glastonbury                        15

2  Outlaws                                         29

3  Talk of the Devil                               41

4  Stones with a Story                             51

5  Liquid Legends                                  61

6  Saints and Martyrs                              75

7  Churches and Monasteries                        83

8  Stately Ghosts and Legends                      93

9  Screaming Skulls and other Oddities            109

10  Ghosts on the Road                            119

11  Hell-hounds and other Pets                    127

12  Odds and Ends                                 139

Sources and Further Reading                       145

Acknowledgements                                  149

Index                                             151

# ILLUSTRATIONS

The Holy Thorn at Glastonbury, Somerset            17
Tintagel Castle, Cornwall                          17
Roman amphitheatre at Caerleon, Monmouthshire      18
Little John's grave at Hathersage, Derbyshire      18
Dick Turpin's house, Thaxted, Essex                35
Robin Hood's Bay, Yorkshire                        35
Cottages at Veryan, Cornwall                       36
Halter Devil Chapel at Mugginton, Derbyshire       36
Crooked spire at Chesterfield, Derbyshire          53
Belfry at Brookland, Kent                          53
The Devil's Chair on Stiperstones Ridge, Salop     54
Lanyon Quoit, Cornwall                             54
Mermaid's Pool at Morridge, Staffordshire          71
Swarkestone Bridge, Derbyshire                     71
The river Trent                                    72
Whitby Abbey, Yorkshire                            72
St Chad's Well, Stowe, Staffordshire               89
St Augustine's Well, Cerne Abbas, Dorset           89
Village sign at Swaffham, Norfolk                  90
The 'Tub' at Beeby, Leicestershire                 90
Astley Castle, Warwickshire                        107
Beaulieu Church, Hampshire                         107
Tunstead Farm, Derbyshire                          108
Rochester Castle, Kent                             108
Lyme Hall, Cheshire                                133
Blickling Hall, Norfolk                            133
Haunted road into Ratlinghope, Salop               134
Purse Caundle Manor, Dorset                        134

The Dun Cow Hotel, Dunchurch, Warwickshire     135
Warwick Castle     135
Lady Godiva's statue at Coventry, Warwickshire     136
Exton Old Hall, Rutland     136

*All the photographs were taken by Frank Rodgers of Allestree, Derby*

# INTRODUCTION

ONE August morning I found myself rather unexpectedly
standing on the end of the escarpment of Edge Hill, not
far from Edge Hill Tower. A mixture of motives had brought
me up there. Partly, I had had enough of traffic on the main
roads and felt a sudden urge to head northwards along the
quieter byways; partly, there had been the feeling that I
ought to look at the site of the battlefield where Royalists and
Parliamentarians had fought their bloody but inconclusive
engagement on an autumn day in 1642. Finally, I was inspired by the description, in the excellent Warwickshire
guidebook I had with me, of the wide views I should enjoy
from the edge of the escarpment.

As it turned out, though I certainly dodged the traffic, I
was thwarted of my other two aims. After more than three
centuries a battlefield looks more or less like any other stretch
of country, and without a large-scale plan of the site I was
little the wiser for my pilgrimage. As for the view, that was
effectively blotted out by a heat haze. In a way I was rather
glad of that haze, if only because it sharpened my imagination. If I could not see the Malvern Hills, the Cotswolds, or
the distant uplands of the Welsh border, as my guidebook
had promised, I could picture them mentally perhaps more
clearly than I should have seen them in a crystalline atmosphere. And as I peered through the haze on that still morning,
my imagination began to tick over.

Somewhere a few miles to the south on the Cotswold
escarpment, were those mysterious Rollright Stones, where
strange things happened at dawn. Further south still was

Oxford, with its dreaming spires and haunted colleges. North-westward was Bidford-on-Avon, where Shakespeare was said to have become uproariously drunk at the Falcon Inn; and Charlcote, where tradition has it that he poached the Lucy's deer. Beyond that was Coventry, where Peeping Tom peered lecherously at Lady Godiva; and Warwick, home of the legendary Guy of Warwick. And closer at hand, beneath the turf, was the Red Horse, a large figure cut into the hillside over a thousand years ago but now hidden below trees and fields. Here I was in the heart of England, surrounded by ghosts and legends. Was I in fact standing on the very road on which the hoof-beats of ghostly cavalry horses can still be heard at night? Should I see through the haze the battle of Edge Hill refought in the sky, as did the villagers of Radway in that Christmas week of 1642, and shortly afterwards the six highly reputable commissioners whom the king sent to investigate the incident?

The prosaic answer must be that I did not of course. But when I drove down from Edge Hill I was acutely aware of how numerous are the legends and ghost stories of Britain. Travelling on through leafy Warwickshire lanes, I decided that I must find out more about these stories and have them at my command whenever I visited an unfamiliar district, for I am with James Boswell in feeling a pleasure in 'walking about any town to which I am not accustomed', and that pleasure is sharpened if I know something of the history, customs, traditions and legends of the place. Of course, the word 'town' includes villages, hamlets and tracts of open country. I am an inveterate explorer, and my exploration is all the more pleasant if I know something of the background of the territory I am exploring. Nowadays towns look increasingly alike. Under the excuse of 'development' there has been a conspiracy to remove all the quirks and eccentricities of place; it is becoming increasingly difficult to detect any difference between, say, Bolton and Bradford. To get any enjoyment out of a place one must know something of its story; be able to say 'this is the house where...', or 'on this hill at midnight on St Swithun's night...'

And so, appropriately near to the centre of England, this book was conceived. Its aims are not particularly ambitious. All I have set out to do is to present to those with a taste for romance a selection of our most interesting legends and ghost stories. Inevitably it can only be a selection or the book would be impossibly long. I hope readers will not feel aggrieved if their favourite stories are omitted. Nor, I trust, will those in Northern Ireland or the Isle of Man take umbrage that their legends—and there are many—are not mentioned; one must stop somewhere.

I have tried to confine myself to stories connected with places that can still be seen. Vague legends and hauntings that have no definite topographical background have been omitted.

First of all, what is a legend? The *Concise Oxford Dictionary* defines it as a 'traditional story popularly regarded as historical myth'. The difficulty with some legends is of separating fact from fiction. Some years ago Sir Robert Birley, then Headmaster of Eton, wrote a pamphlet in which he examined some of our traditional stories, and found it exceedingly difficult either to confirm or discredit them. In such tales as King Alfred and the cakes, and Drake and his famous game of bowls he detected a germ of truth, but thought they had been greatly added to by later chroniclers. On the other hand, he rejected completely the story of Canute and the waves, which will upset the inhabitants of Southampton—particularly those who live in Canute Road—and of Bosham and Grimsby, all of whom regard their native place as the scene of the incident. My own view is that this was a piece of political satire put out by Canute.

However, you will not find in this book scholarly researches into the origins of our legends. Where such research is par-

ticularly interesting I may mention it, and those who wish
to dig more deeply will find a list of sources and suggestions
for further reading at the end of the book. This book is not
primarily intended for scholars; it is aimed at the general
reader who likes to know something of the place he is visiting.
He must generally draw his own conclusions about the truth
of the stories. Some are obviously incredible, others could
well be true; more may have a basis of truth, but have grown
with the telling.

It certainly does not always do to be too scornful of local
legends. Folk memories are astonishingly long. Guy Williams
tells of a field near Mold in north Wales that was believed to
be haunted by 'the ghostly figure of a king or chieftain clad
in golden armour'. Near the end of the nineteenth century
'the body of a Bronze Age chieftain was uncovered in the
field. The chieftain had been buried in a magnificent gold
cape, which is now in the British Museum. His memory had
been perpetuated by word of mouth for close on two thousand
years...' Henry Betts repeats a story told by Arthur Machin
early this century of an interesting conversation with an
Oxfordshire countryman from whom he sought directions to
Chalgrove Field. 'Chalgrove Field,' repeated the farmer,
'that's where Mr Hampden was killed. They do say it was
down in oats at the time.' And 'they' were almost certainly
right, though the history books do no recall the detail.

It is possible, therefore, that behind even the least likely
story there is just a strata of truth, though the actual details
have been altered and probably expanded through many
centuries of telling. Historians tend to discount the story of
Dorothy Vernon's elopement with John Manners from Haddon Hall in Derbyshire on the grounds that the steps down
which she fled, and the bridge where she joined her lover for
their flight to Aylestone in Leicestershire where they were
married, were not built until more than a century after their
marriage. But I certainly cannot see that this utterly dis-

proves the essential validity of the story.

So it is with ghost stories. I am fairly open-minded on this subject. I have never seen one myself, though I think I once heard one, but I am perfectly willing to accept that very odd experiences have befallen people whose integrity is beyond question. Curiously enough, I have just broken off writing to speak on the telephone to a lady whose country mansion 'is absolutely riddled with ghosts'. It is about such houses in which inexplicable things do happen that I am writing here. Not that all such houses are open to the public. But some of them are. You will find an up-to-date list in issues of *Historic Houses, Castles and Gardens in Great Britain and Ireland*. Or you can enquire at the Tourist Information Centre of the British Tourist Authority, 64 St James's Street, London SW1 1NF.

Some of the stories in this book will be fairly familiar. Everybody knows something about King Arthur and Robin Hood, but no book on legends could possibly omit them. Some will be less well known because they have probably never been published before outside their own locality. And others will be entirely new to nearly all readers because they are published here for what I believe to be the first time.

# CHAPTER ONE

# FORWARD FROM GLASTONBURY

ANY search for British legends must begin at Glastonbury, for there is the site of some of the most dramatic and best known of our traditions. It was there that St Joseph of Arimathea planted his staff that grew miraculously into the Holy Thorn; there that the first Christian church was built in Britain; there that St Patrick and St Dunstan were born and buried. It was also the burial place of King Arthur and his Queen Guinevere. All this and the Holy Grail, together with the possibility that it was visited by Christ himself and by St Paul, belongs to Glastonbury. Or so the legends run.

Despite all this, or perhaps because you expect too much, your first impression of Glastonbury may be of slight disappointment. You go there expecting to find a 'many-towered Camelot'—which in fairness it must be said that it has never claimed to be—and find instead a great deal of dull red brick and, on summer weekends, far too much traffic. True, it has the ruins of its abbey, once the largest church in Britain apart from old St Paul's, with the abbot's kitchen remarkably well preserved, a magnificent tithe barn that once belonged to the abbey, the fifteenth-century George and Pilgrims Inn, where they label a lavatory *Necessarium* (or they did when I was last there), a museum of relics from the lake villages of Meare and Godney, and, of course, the Tor. But to appreciate all this, your imagination must first be stirred.

The best way to capture the Glastonbury atmosphere is to see it first from Cadbury Castle, some 12 miles to the southeast. From there, one of the strongest of several claimants to

Page 17 (above) *The Holy Thorn at Glastonbury, Somerset;* (below) *Tintagel Castle, Cornwall, traditional birthplace of King Arthur*

Page 18  (above) *Roman amphitheatre at Caerleon, Monmouthshire, sometimes called King Arthur's Round Table;* (below) *Little John's grave at Hathersage, Derbyshire*

be the original Camelot, on a deep blue afternoon in high summer you will see faintly the Tor, with the vague shape of the ruined chapel of St Michael on its summit, rising sharply from the boggy flat lands, criss-crossed by the polders, or 'rhines', of Sedgemoor. From there it is easy to see Glastonbury as it was—the Isle of Glass, or Avalon, the 'apple orchard', have it which way you will—a true island once surrounded by the sea. Once you have had that memorable view you will go to Glastonbury prepared to ignore its Victoriana and prepared to come to terms with its more remote past and its numerous legends.

Recounting those legends is comparatively easy; sifting out the truth is much harder. For this you must turn to the numerous works on the subject: to Geoffrey Ashe, the late R. F. Treharne, or Desmond Hawkins. All I have space for are the bare bones of the stories.

The legends begin with St Joseph of Arimathea. He it was, the four Gospels agree, who asked Pilate for the body of Christ and laid it in the sepulchre. Later—the year AD63 has been suggested—Philip sent him in charge of a group of twelve apostles to convert the Britons to Christianity. Cornish tradition has it that St Joseph already knew Britain, having visited the island in following his trade as a tinner. Indeed the story goes further. On one of his earlier visits he had brought Jesus with him and taught him to extract tin from wolfram, and had also taken the young Jesus to visit Glastonbury. It was this legend that inspired William Blake's lines 'And did those feet in ancient time, walk upon England's mountains green'. And there are vague stories of a visit from St Paul, landing perhaps at Paulsgrove on the shore of what is now Portsmouth harbour.

But to return to St Joseph. The usual version is that he was swept round the Cornish coast by strong winds and landed in Wales, where he found the natives unfriendly and pressed on into the region ruled over by King Arviragus and not subject

B

to Rome. Arviragus, impressed by St Joseph as a man rather than by his religion, offered him living space on the unpopulated but fertile Isle of Glass.

The pilgrims were almost exhausted when on a late December day they reached a hill close to Glastonbury Tor and now known as Wearyall (or Wirrall) Hill. Here they stopped. St Joseph planted his staff, knelt down and prayed by it. Later the Holy Thorn grew on this spot. Some versions say he also buried the Holy Grail that he had brought with him, causing a blood-red spring (The Chalice Well) to gush out, which the sick later visited to be healed. Near there, St Joseph and his followers settled as hermits, building the first Christian church in Britain, on a site now enclosed in the abbey ruins.

This, then, is the story. What is its truth? Even the best of later scholars are uncertain. The Holy Grail is almost certainly mythical, a combination perhaps of pre-Christian Celtic fable and medieval Christian literary romanticism, though at Nanteos, a house near Aberystwyth, were kept for many years the remains of a wooden vessel, known locally as 'the healing cup of Tregaron', which many people believe to be the Holy Grail. This vessel is now in the possession of Mrs Mirylees of Caple Mead, How Caple, in Herefordshire.

The thorn is real enough: a freak hawthorn that blossoms regularly about the date of old Christmas Day (6 January). Unfortunately there is no written reference to it before 1520, by which time it was admittedly a mature tree, apparently with two trunks. The story of its planting was evidently known by Elizabethan times, for a puritan self-righteously hacked down one trunk. The other trunk is said to have received similar treatment from a Roundhead soldier in the Civil War. In the process he was struck in the eye by a splinter from which he died. But cuttings had been taken from the original tree and these descendants continue to flourish at Glastonbury and elsewhere. In fact Desmond

Hawkins says that the eighteenth-century Bristol merchants worked up a profitable business in selling Holy Thorn sprays, some even going to the export market. He also points out the curious fact that the seeds of the thorn merely produce the common hawthorn. The winter flowering tree comes only by grafting.

But if the Holy Grail is pure fable and the Holy Thorn a natural phenomenon, there seems no doubt about the existence of the original church. It was still there to impress William of Malmesbury in 1120, and was only swept away by the great fire of May 1184 that also gutted the Norman church alongside. This is not to say that the building was necessarily connected with Joseph of Arimathea, if he ever came to Britain at all, or that it was built in the first century. But there seems conclusive proof that it was standing as early as the sixth century, when it was the centre of some sort of rudimentary monastic house.

Whether it was the burial place of Arthur and Guinevere again is doubtful. The originator of the story was Geoffrey of Monmouth, whose entertaining and lively *History of the Kings of Britain* (completed about 1136) sprang mainly from a fertile imagination, with odd snatches of fact thrown in to confuse later historians who have never quite been able to separate the wheat of truth from the chaff of imagination. His story received later support from the more factual Giraldus Cambrensis who said that Henry II had heard from a Welsh bard that Arthur was buried in Glastonbury Abbey. Henry told the abbot, who took no immediate action. Then later, about 1190, the monks got to work and excavated Arthur's body in a huge oak coffin under a stone which was conveniently inscribed with the words (in Latin) 'Here lies buried the renowned King Arthur in the Isle of Avalon'.

So at one turn of the spade 'two truths were told': that Glastonbury was the real Avalon and that the abbey held the bones of Arthur—extremely sizeable bones—and, incidentally, some strands of Guinevere's blonde hair, as well as her bones. The timing of the discovery was providential. It was just six years after the fire, at a time when the abbey urgently needed funds for rebuilding. It provided just the publicity that was wanted.

Many modern historians are inclined to write the find off as an exceptionally able piece of monkish public relations. They accept that there was a stone. It was seen by numerous reliable witnesses before it mysteriously disappeared in the eighteenth century. But there is no certain evidence that it was genuine, and the excavation is generally held to be a clever if not over-subtle fake, though there are those (including Mr Geoffrey Ashe) who are less sceptical.

And this brings us to Arthur. Was he a real king, a legendary folk-hero, or a fictional character from the works of romantic writers like Malory? Modern opinion accepts that essentially he was none of these. He was a genuine historical figure; not a king but a great soldier, a skilled cavalry leader, and a Christian. They accept the opinion of Nennius, writing in the ninth century, that he was one of the last of the great leaders of Romano-British civilisation, successfully withstanding for a time the onslaughts of the pagan Anglo-Saxon invaders. It is suggested that his life spanned a period roughly between 470 and 530.

A belief in the existence of Arthur, who quite possibly held the title of Duke of Britain, does not mean that you have to accept all the stories about him. Numerous legends from folklore and from later literature have become attached to his name. We can safely dismiss Geoffrey of Monmouth's vivid account of Arthur's killing of the lustful giant of St Michael's Mount and the legend of his hurling match with the devil which accounts for the boulders strewn around Hel Tor and other places in Cornwall. If he was not a king, then the story of a coronation, whether at Caerleon-on-Usk, Cirencester, Silchester or Winchester, must go too.

Merlin the magician is another imaginary figure, owing much to the resourceful Geoffrey who well deserves his fifteenth-century memorial oriel window—'Geoffrey's Window'—that can be seen in a school at Monmouth. Merlin certainly did not build Stonehenge with stones he transported from Ireland. That most famous of our prehistoric monuments had stood for 2,000 years before Merlin's supposed birth. He had no connection either with Merlin's Rock, east of Lamorna Cove in Cornwall, nor with the famous oak tree at Carmarthen, whose ancient remains are carefully preserved to prevent the disaster predicted many centuries ago that

When Merlin's tree shall tumble down,
Then shall fall Carmarthen town.

And what of the Round Table and its twenty-four knights? Are they legendary too? Most of them probably are. The Round Table which people flock to see in Winchester Castle was made not earlier than 600 years after Arthur's death—probably later still. Other 'Round Tables', such as the Roman amphitheatre at Caerleon, and the various earthworks and flat-topped stones found as far apart as Cornwall and Cumberland, are equally bogus. And though Sir Bedevere (as Bedwyr) and Sir Kay (as Cei) crop up in early Welsh poetry, Lancelot, Galahad, and several others seem to have been later, fictional characters. On the other hand, Tristan, the lover of Isolde, his uncle's wife, was apparently a real person, though not necessarily connected with Arthur. His monument can still be seen near Fowey. It is a 7ft high standing stone bearing a Latin inscription in fading lettering, 'Here lies Drustans' (Tristan) 'son of Cunomorus'.

That Tintagel was Arthur's birthplace was accepted by all early writers, but though later historians may have their doubts they can offer no suitable alternative. He cannot have been born in the present castle, which is Norman, but he was probably a Westcountryman and the atmosphere of Tintagel is just right.

There is less unanimity about Camelot. Cadbury Castle is a hot favourite, and has been since the sixteenth century when Leland and Camden were both adamant on the subject. They seem to have based their beliefs on the theory that Geoffrey's River Camblam was the little River Cam which runs through Queen Camel, just below the Iron Age fort of Cadbury Castle, and on local tradition.

Local people certainly have no doubt that the steep, flat-topped hill at South Cadbury is the site of Arthur's palace. They used to believe that the hill was hollow. Strange noises could be heard at King Arthur's Well on the north side of the hill when the lid of St Anne's Well on the south side was banged. Ghostly hunting horns wail in the night, and sometimes the clatter of horses' hooves is heard on the rough, steep path that leads down to the village. On Christmas Eve, King Arthur and his knights, with silver-shod horses, ride down the track that the sober Ordnance Survey map marks as 'Arthur's Hunting Causeway' to the spring by Sutton Montis church, a couple of miles or so away across the fields. Leland reported that a silver horseshoe had been found on the track shortly before his visit. More recently—in the 1920s—late on Midsummer Eve, Miss Christina Hole tells us, a woman watched a number of bright lights moving down the hill. She saw the lights come nearer until they were clearly identified as a troop of armed warriors carrying flame-tipped lances and led by an imposing man on horseback. They approached silently—and then vanished. A moment of midsummer madness? I wonder. South Cadbury and the deep lanes around it wear a strangely evocative atmosphere.

Even on a burning summer afternoon such as I encountered on my last visit to Cadbury Castle, it was easy to people the hill with characters from the past, for the excavations that had then only recently started had already revealed evidence that the site had been occupied at various times—if not continuously—from the early Iron Age, or even before, down to the eleventh century. The volunteer diggers, mostly young people under the professional direction of Mr Leslie Alcock, had already produced proof of occupation in the Arthurian period. Other interesting but inconclusive finds were made in the following years, but it is doubtful if archaeological evidence alone will ever be sufficient to provide indisputable proof that this is the site of Camelot.

Meanwhile, there are other claimants. Cornishmen have a reasonable case for saying that the Camblam was their river Camel and that Camelford is the real Camelot. Malory thought it was Winchester, but Caxton placed it at Caerleon. Carlisle folk, with little evidence but much local patriotism, have advanced the claims of their own city.

Modern writers have offered more valid theories. Mr Beram Saklatvala claims that Slack, now a small village near Huddersfield, was the true Camelot. It has a Roman fort lying on the road that linked York with Chester, and here, runs Mr Saklatvala's thesis, was Arthur's northern headquarters, visited, in line with Malory's ideas, only on rare and special state occasions. Captain Harvey Macpherson, after years of exploration and research, identifies Camelot with Camelon, near Falkirk, and says that the Round Table is below Stirling Castle.

There is similar controversy about the twelve vital battles that Arthur fought. The most decisive one, that completely checked the Anglo-Saxon advance, was fought on Mount Badon. It was there that Arthur, carrying a banner bearing the device of the Virgin Mary, led his troops to a great victory.

But where is Mount Badon? Captain Harvey Macpherson says it was Boudon (or Buden) Hill, just north of Linlithgow, a site now marked by numerous earthworks and camps. Human remains found there in the eighteenth century showed evidence of violent deaths. Below this hill stands Cathlaw (*cath* is Gaelic for a battlefield), which suggests that the site was undoubtedly the scene of grim warfare at some period in history. However, Geoffrey Ashe stands firmly in favour of the south-west. After weighing up the claims of Badbury Rings in Dorset and Liddington Camp near Swindon, he inclines towards Liddington as the site of Mount Badon.

And what of Camlan, where Arthur was mortally wounded by his treacherous nephew, Mordred? A strong tradition places it in the water-meadows close to Slaughter Bridge, just outside Camelford, but O. G. S. Crawford suggested that it was the old Roman fort of Camboglanna, now known as Birdoswald, on Hadrian's Wall, no great distance from the splendid castle of Bamburgh on the Northumberland coast, the reputed 'Joyous Gard'.

Similarly, there are rival theories as to where Arthur's sword Excalibur was thrown into the water. Pomparles Bridge (rebuilt in 1912) over the shallow river Brue on the outskirts of Glastonbury is one contender for the honour. Poole Harbour is another. Two others are in Cornwall: Loo Pool near Helston, and Dozmary Pool on Bodmin Moor, which has at least the right sort of remote, eerie atmosphere that one associates with Arthur.

Altogether there are some six hundred places in Britain, mostly in the west and north, that claim some association with Arthur. Many of these derive from folklore, but if he really was Duke of Britain he must have travelled extensively in defence of his native land. It is hardly surprising, therefore, to find him linked with places as far apart as the Cornish fort of Kelliwic and Arthur's Fold near Perth. Glastonbury's claim to be the burial place of Arthur and his queen is disputed by a belief that Guinevere was buried at Meigle in Perthshire, and that Arthur's grave is on Merbach Hill, near Dorstone at the head of the Herefordshire Golden Valley, in a chambered barrow known as Arthur's Stone.

There is also a tradition that Arthur did not die at all, but merely lies asleep in some cave, waiting with his knights for a call to return to the defence of Britain. Local tradition asserts that the cave was discovered by a shepherd under Sewing-shields Crags in Northumberland. Attracted by a faint light from within, he entered the cave and came eventually to a great hall where Arthur and his queen lay sleeping, sur-rounded by their knights and a pack of hounds. On a table were a garter, a sword and a bugle. The shepherd drew the sword and cut the garter, but hadn't the nerve to blow the bugle. At this point, Arthur woke up and delivered himself of these lines:

> O woe betide the evil day,
> When the witless weight was born,
> Who drew the sword, the garter cut,
> But never blew the bugle horn.

Not surprisingly perhaps after that, the whole party resumed their sleep and the shepherd hurried home to spread the news. But neither he nor anyone else has since been able to find the cave.

Similar stories abound elsewhere. Another shepherd in Snowdonia is supposed to have blundered into a cave near the upper end of Llyn Llydaw and disturbed the sleeping occupants by banging his head against a bell. A farmer had an almost identical adventure near Caerleon, while yet another shepherd—this time named as Potter Thompson—found Arthur and his knights sleeping in a cave under the keep of Richmond Castle in Yorkshire. Perhaps because Manchester businessmen are more numerous there than shepherds, Arthur has been allowed to sleep under Alderley Edge in Cheshire, as he has, as far as I know, in two places called Craig-y-Dinas in South Wales, a cave in the Eildon Hills, near Melrose Abbey, and in Arthur's Cave above the Wye near Symond's Yat.

# CHAPTER
# TWO

# OUTLAWS

OF Robin Hood, as of Arthur, it is fairly safe to say that however much blood he may have spilt it was slight compared with the amount of ink that has since been spilt in proving, to hardly anyone's entire satisfaction, that he did or did not live. But whereas Arthur, though shorn of his royal title, has now passed the credibility test, Robin Hood remains an equivocal figure. While writers like J. W. Walker and Valentine Harris have built up a strong case for his existence as an actual historical character, Lewis Spencer and others have dismissed him summarily as an ancient creation of pagan folklore.

I will have nothing to do with this latter view. I was brought up, so to say, with Robin Hood, and to me he remains a real figure whatever the evidence to the contrary may reveal. I was born in a village on the edge of the great Sherwood Forest, which once occupied a fifth of Nottinghamshire and strayed over the boundary into my native Derbyshire. In my godmother's park there was an ancient hollow oak tree in which Robin Hood was reputed to have hidden. There, despite the fence round it that was designed to discourage romantically minded small boys, I used to spend hours being Robin Hood, which accounts for my vested interest in the famous outlaw.

Of course, my tree (or my godmother's) was a mere sapling compared with the mighty Major Oak near Edwinstowe in the heart of Sherwood. It has been claimed that this is the biggest oak in England. True or not, it is a fact that the tree, inevitably a favourite hiding place of Robin Hood, is 30ft in circumference, and its limbs make a ring of about 260ft. Its branches are now held together by steel cables and its trunk is protected by lead as a result of age and weather. But it is still an impressive tree, and when I was last there the lady custodian who collected the fees and sold picture postcards told me that its trunk could hold twelve people at a time, though, I imagine, with the maximum of discomfort.

This part of Sherwood, in the area known as the Dukeries (though all but one of its dukes have now moved away), wears the appearance of a primeval forest, thick with misshapen, dying oaks. One of these, a mile and a half west of the Major Oak, is Robin Hood's Larder, in which Robin is said to have hung his game.

The medieval church of St Mary at Edwinstowe was reputedly the scene of the marriage of Robin Hood and Maid Marian. Alan a Dale's wedding took place either in the tiny chapel at Steetley, a few miles to the west, which Dr Pevsner describes as 'by far the richest example of Norman architecture in Derbyshire', or at Papplewick, nearer to Nottingham. A vaguer tradition—probably due to the association of names —places this marriage ceremony at the even smaller church at Dale Abbey, a few miles north-east of Derby. All these churches are worth seeing for their own sake, especially perhaps the one at Dale Abbey, which is attached to a farmhouse and must be the only church in England to have its pulpit and reading desk to the east of the altar.

Nottingham itself, scene of so many of Robin Hood's exploits, has disappointingly few relics of the outlaw, even though part of its new inner ring-road is called Maid Marian Way. Its castle, from which Robin made his daring escapes, has suffered greatly from fire damage since his day, and is a much less romantic building than is demanded by its legends or its fine site on the top of a red sandstone rock. Just outside its gates is a lively, modern statue of Robin in bronze, which is periodically defaced by vandals, a fate that has escaped the similar statue at Thoresby Hall in the Dukeries, where there is also an elaborately carved chimneypiece with statues in wood of Robin Hood and Little John.

Little John's grave is in Hathersage churchyard in the Derbyshire Peak. Yew trees 10ft apart mark its limits. When the grave was opened in 1784 a thigh bone nearly 30in long was exhumed. The local squire's brother kept this hanging in his house for a time, until he decided it was unlucky and returned it to the parish clerk. It was stolen from the latter by an antiquarian—an unscrupulous lot in those days—and disappeared. Little John's splendid bow of yew, over 6ft long, hung in the chancel of Hathersage Church for many years and is now preserved in Cannon Hall, near Barnsley, whose corporation maintain both house and bow. Around Hathersage the tradition persists that Little John was a local nailer whose name was John Little, and it is recorded that the initials 'J.L.' could still be read on the head and foot stones of the grave as late as 1792.

Robin Hood is supposed to have died at Kirklees Priory, near Brighouse in Yorkshire, whose prioress betrayed him. According to the famous story, he expressed a wish to be buried under the spot where his last arrow fell. This was fired through a window of the gatehouse, which still stands, and a mound on the hillside nearly half a mile away is said to mark his grave, though this would have been a long shot for a dying man. A stone which used to mark the spot is virtually worn away now, chiefly, according to Mr Valentine Harris, because chunks were hacked away by navvies working on the Lancashire and Yorkshire Railway who thought that stone cured toothache and placed bits under their pillows. But the inscription is an eighteenth-century fake.

A bow belonging to Robin Hood was kept at Fountains Abbey until at least 1760, and another was remembered by the late Sir Osbert Sitwell as hanging on the staircase at Barlborough Hall, Derbyshire, in his boyhood.

But who was Robin Hood, if indeed he existed? Both Mr Walker and Mr Harris equate him with Robert Hood, a yeoman whose birth is recorded in the Wakefield Rolls of 1290, and who was living at Wakefield with his wife Matilda in 1316. He may have been the same Robyn Hode who was in the king's service in 1323–4. Mr Walker, on the other hand, has him serving his Lord of the Manor, the Earl of Lancaster, against the king. When the earl lost his head for treason, Robin lost his land and took to the woods as an outlaw. It was in Barnsdale Forest in the West Riding of Yorkshire, now virtually non-existent, that he first settled with his wife, but Sherwood, a few miles away across a stretch of open country, became his headquarters.

Professor J. C. Holt, however, identifies him with another Robert Hood who lived slightly earlier. This one is described in the Pipe Roll of 1230 as a 'fugitive'. Professor Holt thinks he may have been involved in a movement led by Sir Robert Thwing in 1231–2. 'They carried out systematic raids on the property of foreign monasteries, seized their granaries and sold their corn cheaply or even gave it away for the benefit of the many.'

Whoever was the true Robin Hood, there is no doubt that legend has added greatly to his exploits. He certainly could hardly have covered all the ground with which he is now associated, though he may well have visited the places in Nottinghamshire, Derbyshire, and Yorkshire that bear his name.

Derbyshire has a Robin Hood's Cave on Stanage Edge and Robin Hood's Stoop—the base and shaft of a medieval stone cross—on Offerton Moor. Not very far away, on Ludworth Moor, are Robin Hood's Picking Rods, two stones obviously erected by human hands which are said to have been used for bending the bows when stringing them. Further south, near Birchover, is Robin Hood's Stride, a natural pyramid of out-cropping rock. The distance between the two most prominent pinnacles is said to measure the length of the outlaw's stride, but as the distance is 22yd this seems most unlikely. Robin Hood's Wells are common enough, and there is also a Little John's Well, near Longshaw Lodge, not far from Hathersage. In Yorkshire, Robin Hood relics stretch beyond the Wakefield–Barnsdale area. Fountains Abbey is reputed to have been the scene of the famous first meeting between Robin and Friar Tuck, though Nottinghamshire folk are adamant that it took place at Fountain Dale between Blidworth and Harlow Wood in Sherwood. When Yorkshiremen point out the Robin Hood's Well near their Fountains, and another, for good measure, between Doncaster and Weatherby, Nottinghamshire people retort that there is a Friar Tuck's Well in their Fountain Dale and that Will Scarlet was buried in Blidworth churchyard.

Yorkshire has another legend that Robin Hood, when things were getting hot for him round Sherwood, took a job as a deckhand on a fishing boat sailing from Scarborough. Not unnaturally, he was horribly seasick, but managed to recover sufficiently to lead a successful boarding of a French ship and remove its treasure. Just north of Scarborough, the delectable coastal village of Robin Hood's Bay (the 'Bramblewick' of Leo Walmsley's delightful novels) offered refuge to the outlaw when he considered escaping to the continent. Loxley, now a Sheffield suburb, is believed locally to have been his birthplace, a tradition based on the work of some of the early ballad writers.

This part of England was certainly the Robin Hood country, but it is less easy to reconcile him with places much further to the south and west. Worcestershire, for instance, has strong but unlikely Robin Hood traditions, and there is a hill outside Ludlow in Shropshire from which he is supposed to have shot an arrow that landed on the roof of Ludlow church, a mile and a half away. Even further to the south-west, near Otterford on the Somerset–Devon border,

Page 35
(right) *Dick Turpin's house, Thaxted, Essex;* (below) *Robin Hood's Bay, Yorkshire, where the outlaw reputedly hid for a time*

Page 36 (above) *There are no corners to conceal the devil in these cottages at Veryan, Cornwall;* (below) *the tiny semi-detached Halter Devil Chapel at Mugginton, Derbyshire*

two groups of barrows 850ft up on the Blackdowns are known
as Robin Hood's Butts, a title which is shared by other standing stones in various parts of the country.

If folklore and ballad have magnified the Robin Hood
story, one would hesitate to write him off entirely as a legendary figure as does Maurice Keen—rather regretfully, one
feels. Mr Keen produces abundant historical evidence for the
existence of bands of outlaws roaming the country after the
Battle of Evesham, which ended Simon de Montfort's rebellion in 1265, and this may account for the Worcestershire
Robin Hood tradition. Many of these outlaws found sanctu-
ary in the wild hills of Peakland. One of them may have
been Poole, whose hiding place at Buxton, still known as
Poole's Cavern, became one of the traditional 'Seven Won-
ders of the Peak' of which Thomas Hobbes and Charles
Cotton wrote so eloquently. This cave became a favourite
resort of tourists, who until recently queued up to pay their
admission fees at the turnstiles, as they may do again if the
cave becomes part of a proposed country park.

If nothing is known of Poole, there is much historical
evidence, and still more legend, attached to that earlier
figure, Hereward the Wake. His birthplace was the castle on
the western edge of the Fens at Bourne, which has adopted
his coat of arms as the town's arms, and tradition says that
he was buried in the chancel of the church of that pleasant
Lincolnshire town after making his peace with William the
Conqueror. But no trace of his grave has ever been discovered, and of the castle little but evocative mounds remain.
Many Hereward stories closely resemble those told later of
Robin Hood. One example is the tale of his entry into the
Norman headquarters at Brandon in Suffolk disguised as a
potter, and fighting his way out again after being recognised,
just as Robin Hood did at Nottingham Castle. But undoubtedly he did hold out for a long time on the Isle of Ely, though
the story of his betrayal by a treacherous monk may be fiction.

C

Fact and fiction are almost equally difficult to separate in the stories of Dick Turpin, the notorious highwayman, but, unlike Robin Hood and Hereward, he was undoubtedly a thoroughly bad character. He began his 'working' career as a butcher's apprentice, supplementing his income by minor crimes from which he eventually graduated to highway robbery and murder, though ironically it was for shooting at a cockerel that he was finally arrested, and for horse-stealing that he was hanged.

Essex and Yorkshire are the counties to visit for most Turpin relics, though a hat and cloak that are reputedly his can be seen at the George Inn, Huntingdon, and fairly recently another greatcoat of his was found at the Three Tuns Inn at Cambridge. It was at an Essex inn, the Rose and Crown at Hempstead, where his father was landlord, that Turpin was born in 1705, as the parish register records. He is supposed to have lived for a time in nearby Thaxted, in a house close to the ancient Guildhall still known as Turpin's House. Another Essex house associated with the highwayman is Tiptofts, a very old, lonely farmhouse at Wimbish, where he reputedly leaped the triangular moat on his famous Black Bess.

Epping Forest was his chief hide-out, but when that grew too hot to hold him he moved north to Yorkshire, though probably at a more leisurely rate than popular legend, inspired by Harrison Ainsworth's *Rookwood*, credits him with. It was at the Green Dragon Inn, Welton, near Hull, that he eventually gave himself up, under the name of Palmer, without a struggle, under the impression that he faced a trivial charge. After further questioning, he admitted that his real name was Richard Turpin, but added that he was not *the* Richard Turpin but another man of the same name, which sounds like the origin of a well-known music hall joke.

Despite his record, he seems to have been strangely popular. While awaiting trial at York, according to a contemporary newspaper account, 'the whole county have flocked to see him and have been very liberal to him, insomuch as he had Wine constantly before him...and 'tis said the Jailer has made £100 by selling liquors to him and his visitors'. This home from home was the old Debtors' Prison, now part of the York Castle Museum, where the iron bedstead on which he slept and the stone table from which he ate are still preserved. A carved ivory whistle, presented to the chaplain on the gallows in the Knavesmire where he died with 'a great assurance' in April 1739, was stolen from the museum some years ago.

Turpin in death seems to travel nearly as extensively as he did in life. His ghost is said to gallop down Trap's Hill, near Loughton, three times a year. It also appears in some Bedfordshire woods and in Bury Lane on the Bedfordshire–Buckinghamshire border. This lane leads to Watling Street, where he was seen several times in the 1920s on the Warwickshire–Leicestershire border. He is said to haunt the Old Swan Inn at Woughton-on-the-Green, and in recent years has turned up at the Bell Inn at Stilton in Huntingdonshire.

A more static outlaw—almost certainly legendary—was Ippikin, whose headquarters was a cave below a prominent rock on Wenlock Edge in Shropshire, now called Ippikin's Rock. A landslide eventually blocked the cave entrance, imprisoning the outlaw-band and their loot. But tradition says that if you stand on the rock and call

Ippikin, Ippikin,
Keep away with your long chin

his ghost will appear, a golden chain round his neck, and hurl you to your death on the rocks below. I have tried this out, and fortunately for me anyway it failed to work.

# CHAPTER
# THREE

# TALK OF THE DEVIL

WIDELY travelled as King Arthur and Robin Hood seem to have been, even they were less ubiquitous than the devil. Without doubt he is the most common figure in British folklore. Devil's Dykes, Stones, Chimneys, Bridges, Fields and Ditches abound. In Scotland he has a dramatic Beef Tub and an equally spectacular Elbow. There can hardly be a single British county that has not at least one place-name associated with the devil, which is hardly surprising as to our ancestors he was a very real figure, lurking not far over their shoulders.

There are even churches that have surprisingly close links with Satan. The curiously named Halter Devil Chapel, lying between Mugginton and Hulland Ward in a quiet stretch of grassland a few miles north-west of Derby, would not have been built at all but for an unexpected encounter between the devil and a local farmer named Brown in 1723.

Brown, a notoriously heavy drinker, decided one dark night to ride to Derby on a pub-crawl. When his wife pointed out that a thunderstorm was imminent and that he was already in no fit state to be on the road, he replied, 'Ride I will, even if I have to halter the Devil'. Going out to the paddock, he struggled for some minutes without success to put the halter over the horse's head. The reason for his difficulty was suddenly made clear to him when a flash of lightning revealed that the recalcitrant animal had sprouted horns. A second later Brown was struck a violent blow and fell unconscious to the ground.

Mrs Brown, having found him and put him to bed, was

sufficiently tactful to avoid pointing out that he had tried to
halter a cow, which, not unnaturally resentful, had kicked
him, and Brown remained convinced that he really had tried
to halter the devil. Taking this as a warning, he gave up
drink and built a chapel attached to the farm, one of the
few semi-detached churches—along with the one at Dale
Abbey mentioned in the previous chapter—in which Angli-
can services are still held. It must also be one of the smallest,
measuring a mere 14ft by 13ft.

The story seems to be substantially true. When the house
was rebuilt nearly a century ago, a tablet bearing the following inscription was lost:

> Francis Brown in his old age
> Did build him here an hermitage        1723
> Who being old and full of evil
> Once on a time haltered the Devil

The register of Mugginton Church, in recording Brown's
death, notes that he founded the 'Chappel in ye Intakes
Hull'd Ward'.

There are other devil stories linked with churches. Though
Chesterfield's famous crooked spire probably acquired its
shape because the lead was too heavy for the unseasoned
timber, a more popular version is that the devil was resting
unnoticed on the spire when he saw a beautiful virgin enter
the church in her wedding dress. In his surprise, he twisted
round, taking the spire with him.

A rather similar story accounts for the leaning detached
belfry at Brookland on Romney Marsh, which has been
likened to 'a three-storied Chinese pagoda'. The steeple
apparently fell off the church in astonishment on seeing a
Brookland couple troubling to go through the formality of a
marriage ceremony. Though the devil is not involved in this
story, he has been blamed for the position of the detached
bell cage in the churchyard at East Bergholt, John Con-
stable's birthplace. The bells should have hung in the tower,

but each night the devil threw down the part of the church tower that the masons had erected during the day. Eventually the workmen accepted the inevitable and put the bells in the timber cage in which they now stand. Another, more likely, story is that the building of the tower was begun at Cardinal Wolsey's expense in 1525 to compensate for the suppression of Dodnash Priory, which caused some financial loss to the parish, and stopped abruptly with the disgrace and death of the Cardinal five years later.

Not long after that, on an August Sunday in 1557, the devil is said to have ridden into the church at Blythburgh, one of the most magnificent of the numerous splendid Suffolk churches, on a storm so fierce as to bring down the spire. On leaving the church, he touched the door and scorched it, leaving a mark that can still be seen. The collapse of the church tower at Widecombe, Devon, in 1638, resulting in the death of four people, was caused by lightning, but local legend has it that it was due to the devil hitching his horse to the tower while he had a drink.

The devil was only indirectly responsible for the demolition of the Norman church at Shobdon in Herefordshire. Because the villagers had boasted that it was the finest church in England, the devil set out to destroy it, but on his arrival he was told by the local cobbler that he was in the wrong village and went away. Before he could return, the villagers pulled the church down themselves. So runs the legend. The truth is that the lord of the manor demolished the church, re-erecting parts of it in his park, where it can still be seen, and replaced it in 1753 with a fantastic rococo church more in keeping with his own architectural fancies.

The devil is also associated with the church in the Worcestershire village of Ripple, well worth a visit for the sake of its sixteen misericords. The door leading out of the chancel, now usually called the Priest's Door, was known until recent times as the Devil's Door because of the pre-Reformation superstition that the devil escaped from the church through it at the elevation of the Host.

If you want to meet old Lucifer himself, there is just a chance that you will if you go up at night on to the ridge running between Thorncombe and Birdsmoor Gate in Dorset. Along there are three widely spaced clumps of trees known as the Devil's Three Jumps. The story runs that on certain nights of the year the devil is seen jumping from clump to clump, but nobody seems to know whether these athletic performances are based on a regular time schedule or just carried out when the old man feels the need for violent exercise. Indeed, one version has it that the jumps were only performed once, when the Abbot of Forde kicked him off his land.

This reminds me of the encounter between St Dunstan and the devil, which is illustrated in the fourteenth-century Luttrell Psalter and in a window of the Bodleian Library at Oxford. There are several versions of the incident. My favourite one says that St Dunstan, then working as a smith, had his forge in a cave at Mayfield in Sussex, where Satan came to tempt him in the form of a beautiful girl. But St Dunstan, who was apparently prepared for the visit, seized the devil by the nose with a pair of red-hot tongs. The pain caused the devil to roar so loudly as to split into three pieces the rock in which the cave was situated and then to jump as far as Tunbridge Wells, where he landed so violently as to cause a spring to flow, which accounts rather pleasantly for the chalybeate spring to which the town owes its fame as a spa. An eighteenth-century writer said that the tongs used in the fight were then still preserved in Mayfield Church, but I am bound to record that the incident is also said to have occurred at Glastonbury, where St Dunstan was born and was to become abbot.

Another encounter with the devil took place in Cardinganshire and led to the building of the famous Devil's Bridge over the river Mynach, near its confluence with the Rheidol. There are actually three bridges close together, the oldest— a twelfth-century structure—being the Devil's Bridge. It was built by the devil to allow a local woman to recover a cow which had somehow strayed on to the wrong side of the gorge. In return for his courtesy, the devil demanded the first living thing to cross the bridge, assuming that it would be the woman herself. But being too shrewd to be so easily caught, she threw over a crust of bread which her dog raced across to collect.

An almost identical legend accounts for the lovely, three-arched bridge over the River Lune at Kirkby Lonsdale in Westmorland, which is now preserved as an ancient monument. When a new bridge was built for traffic 150yd downstream in 1932, the devil was so enraged that he hampered construction by floods and marred the opening ceremony by organising a violent thunderstorm accompanied by hail and snow. So a new twist is added to an old legend.

A lesser known Devil's Bridge, over the little River Dibb in Wharfedale, displays the devil in a more benevolent mood. He met a shoemaker named Ralph Calvert picnicking near the river on his way back to his home village of Thorpe from Fountains Abbey, where he had taken some newly repaired shoes. After inviting himself to share the meal, the devil announced his true identity. Calvert, a sceptical Yorkshireman who no doubt suspected the stranger of being an effete southerner up to some stupid trick, said he would believe him only if his guest would bridge the beck. The devil calmly replied that a bridge would be there in three days, and sure enough it was. There it still is, though it has been rebuilt by human hands, and most maps prosaically call it Dibble's Bridge, assuming that it takes its name from the river.

Few people would face the devil with the confidence of Calvert or St Dunstan. Fear of him remained very real until well into the last century, especially in the more remote parts of Britain. This fear is exemplified by the conically-roofed round houses at Veryan, in that charmingly named part of Cornwall known as Roseland. Originally there were five of these, two at each end of the village and one in the middle. They were built early in the nineteenth century by a Lostwithiel builder at the instigation of the Reverend Jeremiah Trist, vicar of Veryan (1782–1829) as an endowment for his five daughters. Local tradition insists that he built them round to allow the devil no corner to hide in and to make him dizzy if he searched for one. As a further precaution, a cross was erected at the apex of each thatched roof. These whitewashed cottages still stand, along with two more built in 1955 for seamen's widows. Except that they are roofed with the local Delabole slate, the new cottages are replicas of the original round houses, embodying the same precautions against the devil, even to the cross on the roof.

Further east, off Teignmouth on the South Devon coast, are the two prominent red rocks known as the Parson and Clerk Rocks. They are said to be a clergyman and his parish clerk who, after getting lost on a wild night, took refuge in an inn where they joined the locals in drinking and singing bawdy songs, after which the devil, in the guise of the innkeeper, offered to lead them on their way, took them into the sea and then turned them to stone.

This story is typical of many which sprang up to account for unusual geological features. Our primitive ancestors, lacking scientific knowledge, were apt to attribute such phenomena to the devil. Thus Filey Brigg, that long reef on the Yorkshire coast, is supposed to be the devil's handiwork, and Stanner Rocks, near Kington, said to be the only place in fertile Herefordshire where nothing will grow, was the devil's garden. A pile of granite slabs on Bodmin Moor is known as the Devil's Rocking Chair, and the highest point on the Stiperstones Ridge in Shropshire (1,741ft) is the Devil's Chair, 'a mass of quartzite, blackened and hardened by uncountable ages', as Mary Webb described it in *Golden Arrow*. The loose stones around it are supposed to have spilled from the devil's apron when he rose abruptly from the chair, to which he is said to return occasionally. If any human sits on it, a thunderstorm breaks out immediately.

In Shropshire another spectacular work of the devil is the Wrekin. It was formed when he set out to dam the Severn, so causing a flood that would drown the town of Shrewsbury, against which he had a special grudge. For this purpose he carried a giant spadeful of earth, which he found extremely heavy. On meeting a cobbler with a sackful of shoes for repair slung over his shoulder, he asked the distance to Shrewsbury. The cobbler—cobblers seem to have been remarkably astute in dealing with Satan—recognised his questioner, thought quickly, and remarked that he had just come from that town, which was so far away that he had worn out the sackful of shoes on the walk. The devil despairingly threw down his load of earth, which became the Wrekin, and then scraped his boots on his spade, thus forming the smaller Ercall Hill close by.

Almost identical stories are told of a mound called The Devil's Spadeful at Bewdley and of the famous Silbury Hill, while a rather similar one explains the green bowl known as the Hole of Horcum and a hill called Blakey Topping on the Yorkshire Moors. These features were formed when the devil, intending to bury Scarborough, dropped the spadeful of earth he had just dug up on being startled by the sun shining on Lilla Cross.

Another Yorkshire place to incur the devil's displeasure was Aldborough near Boroughbridge. Intending to destroy the township, he fired four giant arrows from Howe Hill, near Fountains Abbey. Fortunately, the devil's arrows fell a mile or so short of their target, where three of these immense stones still stand not far from the Great North Road. The fourth one was broken up some three centuries ago to build a nearby bridge. Another great monolith, in the churchyard at Rudston near Bridlington, is reputedly an arrow fired at the church by the devil, but like that curious sarsen stone on the Marlborough Downs near Fyfield that is called the Devil's Den, these stones were obviously put there by Neolithic man.

Not all devil stories go back to ancient folklore. His most spectacular manifestation occurred as recently as February 1855, when he left his hoofprint—about $2\frac{1}{4}$ in across—over 100 miles of snow-covered Devon. These prints were not confined to the ground, but crossed roofs and ran along walls. For days afterwards, people stayed indoors and parsons explained the phenomenon from their pulpits, but the mystery has never been entirely cleared up, though many scientists are inclined to accept the rather unromantic theory advanced by an Essex naturalist, Alfred Leutscher, that the prints were made by wood mice seeking shelter.

# CHAPTER
# FOUR

# STONES WITH A STORY

NOT all standing stones or curious rock formations are associated with the devil. The famous Rollright Stones, for instance, on the Oxfordshire–Warwickshire border, are the remains of an early Bronze Age stone circle, but popular legend attributes them to the machinations of a witch. The circle itself consists of more than sixty badly weathered and generally unimpressive stones occupying a space not more than 100ft in diameter, though it may once have been larger. These stones are called the King's Men because they are said to have been the followers of a king who was leading them into battle when the witch turned them into stone. About a quarter of a mile eastward are four upright stones called the Whispering Knights because they were four knights who had stayed apart from the main army to plot against the king and were similarly changed to stone for their treachery. The king, meanwhile, had gone forward at the suggestion of the witch, who told him

Seven long strides shalt thou take,
And if Long Compton thou canst see
King of England thou shalt be.

As the village of Long Compton was no great distance away and should have been easily visible from the edge of the ridge, the king eagerly took his seven long strides, only to have his view blocked by a mound which disconcertingly sprang up before him, whereupon the witch turned him into stone and herself into an elder tree, a fairly common if some-what puzzling practice of witches that was possibly linked with the belief that Judas hanged himself from an elder.

(right) *Legend blames the devil for this famous crooked spire at Chesterfield, Derbyshire;* (below) *the leaning, detached belfry at Brookland, Kent*

Page 54 (above) *The Devil's Chair on Stiperstones Ridge, Salop, 'blackened and hardened by uncountable ages'*; (below) *Lanyon Quoit, Cornwall*

Incidentally, it is supposed to be impossible to count the Rollright Stones, just as it is with the Countless Stones close to Kits' Coty House, a mile or so from Aylesford in Kent. A local baker, who tried to settle the matter by placing a loaf on each stone, lost his reason after finding himself a loaf short.

Many standing stones are said to have been people who were guilty of working, or, even worse, of enjoying themselves, on the Sabbath. The best known of these stories concerns the group of stone circles at Stanton Drew in Somerset known as The Fiddlers and the Maids. The tradition is that a bridal couple and their guests were celebrating the marriage by dancing there on the Saturday night of their wedding. At midnight the fiddler, who had been providing the music, refused to continue playing because of his religious scruples. The bride indignantly demanded more music, saying, according to some accounts, that she would go to hell to find another musician if necessary. The deadlock was broken when a bearded old man appeared and offered to play, though his first pieces were too mournful to satisfy the dancers. When they protested, he stepped up the tempo so that they whirled round at a dizzy pace until they could not stop. In the morning they and the fiddler—our old friend the devil perhaps—were all found turned to stone.

Almost identical stories explain many other groups of stones, especially in Devon and Cornwall. By way of variation, the remains of three stone circles on the moors above Liskeard were once men who took part in the traditional Cornish sport of hurling on a Sunday. One version has it that St Cleer warned them against this transgression of the Sabbath and was promptly told that they would stay there for ever. These circles are known as the Hurlers.

A similar fate overtook three women who insisted on winnowing corn on the summit of Penmaenmawr on a Sunday. They remain there as three upright stones of different colours—patriotically red, white and blue—which are

D

said to be the colours of the gowns worn by the women at the time of their dramatic transition.

An act of meanness was responsible for the large stones called the Grey Geese that litter a hill at Edward Thomas's Adlestrop. A woman taking her geese to market was stopped by a witch who asked for money. When this request was refused, the witch turned the geese into stones.

Witches did not always have things their own way. Long Meg and her Daughters, at Little Salkeld near Penrith, were witches who were themselves turned to stone. The Daughters form a stone circle—countless, of course—about 30yd from Long Meg, a larger block of sandstone, the 'giant-mother' whose 'massy strength and stature' inspired a Wordsworth sonnet.

Some standing stones have been explained away as the playthings of giants. A race of giants, who inhabited south-west Cornwall, tossed around the various 'quoits' that stand on the hills at Zennor, Lanyon and other places in the area. Hauteville's Quoit, near Stanton Drew, was reputedly thrown by Sir John Hauteville, a local giant, from Maes Knoll on the other side of the River Chew. Sir John was a genuine medieval character, and as he was apparently a man of great strength and stature his name has probably been super-imposed on a much earlier story, just as the de la Beche family, noted for their size, have become mixed up with the story of a race of giants at Aldworth on the Berkshire Downs.

The Bambury Stone, looking vaguely like a baby bear, on Bredon Hill in Worcestershire, was the result of giants tossing boulders at each other. A couple of giants were responsible for the cliffs at Avon Gorge. In a violent quarrel they threw stones at one another across the river. One of these giants, Goram, has left his footprints in Blaise Castle Woods on the Somerset side of the river, and his chair is a rock just above the river, while there is a Giant's Cave, later used as a hermitage, high up in the cliffs below Clifton Observatory.

Many standing stones are thought to behave oddly at times. Colwall Stone, below the whale-back of the Malverns, is supposed to turn completely round when the clock strikes midnight, while the Nine Maidens at Belstone, Devon, dance daily at noon. The granite Longstone, above Chagford, is believed to turn slowly round at sunrise to warm each side in turn, while at the same time of day the stones of Grey Wethers, one of the two largest stone circles on Dartmoor, take a short walk.

Other stones, including most rocking stones, used to be thought to have healing powers. To pass three times between the King Stone and Queen Stone on Bredon Hill was a panacea for all ills. The Drake (or Draag) Stone on Harbottle Hill in Northumberland was equally effective in curing children's ailments, but as the stone is 27ft high and the child had to be passed over the top it could hardly have been a simple cure. Equally complicated was the cure for lumbago and rheumatism effected by crawling on all fours nine times —against the sun—through the hole in the Cricker Creeping Stone at Madron, Cornwall, where there is also another stone, called the Men-an-Tol, which cured children who were passed through the hole in its centre.

The welfare state has rendered such uncomfortable cures redundant, and in these mechanised days there is probably less demand for the services of Wayland, the mythical smith or farrier. This character, who probably came to Britain from Norse mythology, will shoe a horse overnight if sixpence or the equivalent value in corn is left under a stone outside Wayland Smith's Cave, a long barrow on the Berkshire Downs.

This area is rich in legends. Only a few miles from Wayland Smith's Cave is the Blowing Stone, which stood some 700ft up on the Ridgeway when Thomas Hughes wrote of it in the opening chapter of *Tom Brown's Schooldays*. But about 1880 an enterprising, energetic but misguided innkeeper rolled it downhill into the garden of his pub in the village of Kingston Lisle, where his customers could amuse themselves by blowing into the stone without the trouble of climbing the hill. The stone has holes at the top and at the sides near the bottom. If you cover the smallest hole completely with your mouth you may with difficulty produce 'a grewsome noyse between a mowne and a roare' which can be heard a mile away. The range may have been as much as 6 miles when it stood on higher ground. King Alfred is said to have used it to summon his army for the Battle of Ashdown in 871, which accounts for its alternative name of King Alfred's Bugle Horn. It should be added that the innkeeper's vandalism evidently did him no good, for the inn has now been replaced by cottages.

Between Wayland Smith's Cave and the Blowing Stone, below the Uffington White Horse, is Dragon Hill, where St George reputedly slew the dragon, whose blood ran downhill, leaving a trail of barren ground on which no grass has since grown, though Herefordshire people claim that the dragon was killed in their county at Brinsop.

A hill with a grimmer tradition is Raggedstone Hill on the Malverns, which owes its name to its irregular rocky summit. Occasionally and quite unpredictably the rock throws a shadow over the valley to the east, and it is said that anyone caught in this shadow is likely to suffer misfortune or even death. It is strongly believed locally that the shadow fell upon Cardinal Wolsey when he was staying at Birtsmorton Court, nearby. Tradition has it that the curse was laid down by a monk of Little Malvern Priory who was forced as a penance to crawl daily on hands and knees from the foot of the Raggedstone to the summit and then pray for forgiveness, but it is more likely that the story goes back to pre-Christian times and is associated with human sacrifice.

Three memorial stones on Whitcliffe Scar, 200ft above the Swale near the Yorkshire Richmond, tell a rather happier story. They mark the leaps made by a horse ridden by Robert Willance which went over the cliff edge in fog in 1606. Though the horse was killed, Willance escaped with a broken leg to erect the stones inscribed with the words: '1606, Glory be to our merciful God who miraculously preserved me from the danger so great'.

If the story of Willance's Leap is true, that of Wintour's Leap at Tidenham in Gloucestershire seems less probable. This man Wintour, escaping pursuit, deliberately rode his horse over the edge of a precipice and got away by swimming the Wye. Equally unlikely is the tale of Jock's Leap at Aydon, Northumberland. Jock was one of two Scottish raiders captured by Sir Robert Claver and condemned to death by being thrown from the roof of Aydon Castle into the Cor Burn below. He saved his life, tradition says, by a prodigious jump across the burn.

Many counties have similar leap stories; many have yarns like the one that accounts for St Leonard's Cross at Thrybergh. This romantic tale tells of a Leonard de Reversby who went off to fight in the Crusades, leaving at home a beautiful young wife. Leonard was taken prisoner and was unable to get any word home to his wife. She waited patiently for seven years, but then, his death being presumed, she reluctantly agreed to marry again, though praying that her husband might yet return. This he did, still shackled, being found alive in Thrybergh Field just as the wedding party was on its way to church. The cross, of which now only the shaft remains, was set up on the spot where he was found, but has now been moved to the old churchyard as a safeguard against vandalism.

This story reminds me of another one of a wedding that was hurriedly cancelled at the last minute. This concerns Elizabeth Sydenham, Sir Francis Drake's fiancée. During one of his long voyages she despaired of his ever returning, and accepted a less peripatetic suitor. When the wedding day arrived she was on her way to church when what appeared to be a cannon ball fell in front of her. Accepting this as a gentle rebuke from Drake for her impatience and lack of faith, she cancelled the wedding and waited for the return of her original fiancé, who soon arrived to marry her. This missile, actually a piece of a meterorite shaped like a cannon ball, is still retained, I believe, at Combe Sydenham Hall in Devon.

# CHAPTER
## FIVE

# LIQUID LEGENDS

STORIES of lost lands under the sea are amongst the oldest legends in the world. Atlantis, somewhere beneath the Atlantic Ocean, has been the subject of learned works as well as providing plots for adventure stories for both children and adults. Plato mentions that it was destroyed by the sea because of the wickedness of its inhabitants.

Lyonesse has a more localised reputation. It allegedly lay off the coast of Cornwall and may indeed have formed part of that county. It crops up regularly in Cornish and Breton folklore. According to some legends it was the land of Arthur and included his Camelot.

Whatever truth there may be about these lost lands, there is no doubt about the existence of the Goodwin Sands, some 6 miles or so off the Kent coast at Deal. During World War 2 their boundaries were clearly marked by a line of masts of sunken ships sticking up out of the water like the topmost branches of some submerged forest. Legend has it that the Goodwins once formed the island of Lomea belonging to Earl Godwin who died in 1035. He is supposed to have given money to an abbot of St Augustine's, Canterbury, for the purpose of building a sea-wall, but the man of God decided that the money would be better used to build a fine steeple on Tenterden Church. The result was that Lomea was inundated, giving rise to the saying that 'Tenterden Steeple was the cause of the Goodwin Sands', though Richard Church believed the Lomean story to be a garbled version of that of Earl Godwin's Isle of Thanet, which has now become part of the mainland.

Another legend attributes the formation of the Goodwin Sands to the earl's failure to honour a pledge to take Holy Communion daily. As a result the sea swallowed much of his Kentish possessions, leaving only parts of the Goodwins visible at low tide. The Godwin Cup, from which he was to take Communion, is still on view at Berkeley Castle in Gloucestershire. The Manor of Berkeley was part of Earl Godwin's property in Edward the Confessor's reign, though a smaller house stood on the site of the present castle.

The monastery and cathedral of Selsey—the Island of Seals —founded by St Wilfred, have long since been engulfed by the sea. In St Wilfred's time—around AD700—it was not quite an island, being 'compassed around by the sea except on the west side, where it had an entry into it of about a stone's throw', according to Bede, but this entry was gradually eaten away until in 1075 the cathedral had to be resited at Chichester. But as late as the reign of Elizabeth I, Camden said that at low water it was 'evident and plaine to be seen'. Hilaire Belloc, in his charming essay 'The Looe Stream', says 'In Henry VIII's time there was still a park left out of the old estates'; you will still find 'The Park' marked on charts of the English Channel, along with the Looe stream, the 'little dell that used to run through that park'. While sweeping that area for mines during World War 2, I thought I had proved the truth of the legend that the bells of Selsey Cathedral could still be heard under the water, but the sound turned out to come from nothing more romantic than a barnacle-encrusted bell-buoy.

Traditions of towns under the sea around our coast are numerous. Some are true. The Ravenspur of Shakespeare's *Richard II*, where Henry Bolingbroke 'with uplifted arms is safe arriv'd' to seize the crown of Henry IV, certainly existed just eastward of Spurn Head, and it is well known that Dunwich, further down the east coast, is only a remnant of a busy medieval port which had five churches. Other tales are more doubtful. Did Kilgrimod, near Blackpool, really exist? Do Church Rocks, off Cromer, really mark the site of Cromer's original church, as tradition insists?

The story of Llys Helig, a palace whose walls can still be seen at the lowest tides some 2 miles out to sea in Conway Bay, seems to have been knocked on the head by F. J. North. The palace was reputedly that of a Welsh king, Helig ap Glannawg (or Glannog), who lived at some vague date between the fifth and eighth centuries. He seems to have been an unpleasant person, and according to legend (of which there are numerous versions) it was prophesied that his palace and lands would be swallowed up four generations later. This suspended sentence, which probably did not worry Helig overmuch, duly came about. But Mr North, after a careful survey by boat, has found that the 'palace walls' are no more than boulders of glacial origin, and his equally thorough search of the documentary evidence has demolished the story as effectively as the sea has reputedly demolished the 'palace'.

Not all stories of submerged church bells that can be heard ringing in wild weather or at Christmas time are attributed to drowned villages. Off Whitby, the original bells of the abbey can still be heard under the sea, and any lover whispering the name of his or her sweetheart on looking out to sea on All Saints' Eve will hear them ringing a marriage peal. There are two slightly differing versions of the story of how the bells came to be under the sea. One version says that the bells were sold at the Dissolution of the Monasteries and were being transported to London by sea when the ship carrying them was becalmed, and then, astonishingly, sank for no apparent reason within sight of the abbey. The other version has it that it was the Danes who were carrying off the bells. It was certainly the Danes who threw the bells of Bosham Church into that lovely little Sussex harbour in a place still known as Bell Creek.

Bells can often be heard ringing at the bottom of many of

our lakes, which seem to be cluttered up with lost towns, villages, and palaces. The story of old Bala that now reputedly lies beneath Bala Lake was told to George Borrow so graphically by a Welsh lad he met by the side of the lake that it cannot be improved upon. 'It stood,' said the lad, 'in the old time where the lake now is, and a fine city it was, full of fine houses, towers and castles, but neither church nor chapel, for the people neither knew God nor cared for Him, and thought of nothing but singing and dancing and other wicked things. So God was angry with them, and one night, when they were all busy at singing and dancing and the like, God gave the word and the city sank down into the Unknown, and the lake boiled up where it once stood.'

There is some similarity in the story of Semer Water (spelt in various ways) in the North Riding of Yorkshire that inspired James Kirkup's first poem. Here a ragged old tramp is supposed to have sought hospitality, but to have been turned away from every door until he reached a shepherd's hovel on the hillside. There he was welcomed, invited to stay the night and share what little there was to eat. Having thanked the shepherd and his wife and given them a blessing, he unexpectedly changed into a well-dressed young man who promptly put a curse on the village in the valley. Immediately a storm arose, flooded streams poured into the valley, and the next morning the village had disappeared under the waters of the newly formed lake. Only the shepherd's hovel on the hillside remained above water. A ruined cottage there is said to be the original one. This story, as Henry Betts reminds us, is almost identical with that of Baucis and Philemon, who were the only people to offer hospitality to Zeus and Hermes when they returned to earth in human shape, with the result that their home was the only one to escape when the angry gods flooded the valley.

But an historical explanation may possibly account for the story of the city that is reputed to lie below Llangorse Lake, between Brecon and the Black Mountains. It was this lake that was said by Giraldus Cambrensis, writing late in the twelfth century, to be 'sometimes seen by the inhabitants covered and adorned with buildings, pastures, gardens and orchards', and when it was frozen over to emit 'a horrible sound resembling the moans of many animals collected together'. Gerald's leg may have been gently pulled, but more recent finds under the lake have given rise to a theory that the legend is based on folk-memories of a lake-village, like those near Glastonbury, that was inundated during a gale, for the lake is subject to violent winds.

Most of the meres of Cheshire and Shropshire have their legends, usually variations of the Llys Helig or Semer Water stories. Bomere Pool, just south of Shrewsbury, was formed, it is said, when a dam collapsed one Christmas Eve, drowning the notoriously godless village there. Through a gross miscarriage of justice even the parish priest, who had predicted some such disaster if the people did not mend their ways quickly, perished with his flock as he was ringing the sanctus bell in the church. The bell can still be heard faintly below the waters on Christmas Eve. Not far to the north, under the waters of Cross Mere, the church bells of another drowned village can be heard any time when wind disturbs the lake.

Rostherne Mere, in Cheshire, now a nature reserve, is yet another lake containing a submerged bell. This one was a particularly heavy new bell intended for the parish church. When it was being hauled past the mere on its way to the church the rope broke and the bell was lost in the water, an accident attributed to the strong language used by the workmen.

Variations of this story are repeated in many counties. Northumberland has a tradition of several men and oxen being drowned in Cypher's Linn, a deep pool on the River Allen, when they were trying to recover a box of gold that the friars of nearby Staward had hidden at the Dissolution.

The box was located, the oxen yoked to it, but when they tried to heave up the treasure, animals and men were all swept into the Linn. Whether the men used Anglo-Saxon four-letter words, or whether they were punished for greed, I do not know, but it does appear that many of these legends were made up by earnest Christians as a warning to the ungodly. Typically, one of the many traditions concerning the group of pools known as Hell Kettles, between Croft and Darlington, is that they hide the body of a farmer who insisted on gathering hay on St Barnabas Day; his horse and waggon being down there with him.

If many such legends have Christian foundations, those of mermaids in lakes must be relics of the older pagan belief in water-gods. Many such traditions have survived. Aqualate Mere, near the Shropshire Newport, has a slightly disgruntled mermaid. Not only did she have to move there from Vivary Pool when the Shropshire Union Canal was cut through the pool in the eighteenth century, but she was again disturbed when her new home was being dredged and cleaned more recently. This time she is reputed to have popped her head out of the water and warned the workmen quite firmly that

If this mere you do let dry,
Newport and Meretown I will destroy.

Since then she has been allowed to rest undisturbed.

An even less likely hide-out for a mermaid is the lonely pool which the Ordnance Survey maps unromantically call Blakemere, 1,400ft up on the wild moors near Leek in Staffordshire. Locally it is called Mermaid's Pool, and the lonely inn nearby is the Mermaid Inn. Verses carved on its stonework say that

She calls on you to greet her, combing her dripping crown,
And if you go to meet her, she ups and drags you down.

Apparently she appears at midnight to entice any man stupid enough to be on the moors at this time. The origin of the story is unknown, but it could be explained by the boggy nature of the ground thereabouts, and it does seem to be a fact that the pool has been the scene of one murder and one attempted murder.

Naturally enough, most mermaids are to be found in the sea. One was responsible for silting up Padstow Harbour as an act of revenge because a man had shot at her. Another, for no apparent reason, caused the village of Seaton, near Looe (not to be confused with the Devon Seaton) to be overwhelmed by sand. A third mermaid appears at Mermaid's Rock near Lamorna Cove before a storm, and is heard singing before a ship is wrecked. But the best known of these fairly numerous Cornish mermaids is the one at Zennor, whose figure is carved on a bench-end in the parish church. She is supposed to have been enchanted by the singing of a chorister named Matthew Trewhella, and to have swum repeatedly up the small stream from the sea to listen to his voice. Eventually she enticed him into the sea and he was never seen again, though for many years afterwards his voice could be heard in Pendour Cove when he sang to his mermaid bride.

A sequel to this story has it that some years after Trewhella's disappearance a mermaid put her head out of the water to complain to a local fishing skipper that he had thoughtlessly dropped anchor across the entrance to her home. The skipper obligingly weighed anchor and returned to Zennor to earn a few pints out of his story.

Mermaid stories are fairly common on the Celtic coasts of Britain: Cornwall, Wales and the Scottish isles; they are very rare on the east coast. Yet there is a well-documented story of a 'merman' who spent 'many days and nights' ashore at Orford in Suffolk in the twelfth century. He was described by the Monk Ralph de Coggershall, writing some two centuries later, as 'a wild man' who was caught in the nets of some fishermen and brought ashore. 'He was covered with hair and had a long and shaggy beard', ate well but refused to speak and 'showed no sign of reverence or belief' when taken to church. He was detained in Orford Castle for some time, but though tortured, he willingly returned from a swimming expedition after slipping under the net that guarded him. 'But later on,' wrote his chronicler, 'being negligently guarded, he secretly fled to the sea and was never afterwards seen.' But he has certainly been remembered, thanks partly to Holinshed, who added further details in the sixteenth century. Ralph de Coggershall wondered if the creature was a 'mortal man, or a fish simulating the human species, or some malignant spirit concealed in the body of a drowned man'. Curiously enough, he did not suggest the merman theory—that was left to later writers—nor did he dare to imply that these sturdy east coast fishermen had failed to recognise a seal.

Just as some mermaids entice their victims into the water, so do the water spirits who infest many of our lakes and rivers. One of these is Jenny Greenteeth, a restless character who inhabits many different northern waters, waiting to lure to destruction any who venture too near. Peg Powler, a green-haired spirit, does the same on the Tees. The Dart, the Spey, the Wye and the Tweed all have spirits that demand one sacrifice a year. Peg O'Nell in the River Ribble, on the other hand, is satisfied with one victim every seven years, but the Trent, in its less 'smug and silver' aspect, has a greedier spirit who claims three bodies annually.

It was possibly this spirit who was indirectly responsible for the building of Swarkestone Bridge over the Trent near Derby, and the causeway—three-quarters of a mile long—across the river's flood-plain. Two young ladies, it is said, saw their lovers drowned in attempting to cross the ford there, and devoted the rest of their lives and money to building a bridge so that others might be spared this fate. The story has never been disproved, though it is more likely that the bridge and causeway—parts of which date from the twelfth century

—were built by the monks of Repton, a few miles away.

A rather similar story accounts for the two stone effigies now preserved in a panel on the new South Petherton bridge over the River Parrett in Somerset, having been transferred from the older bridge that was replaced in a road-widening operation in 1971. They are supposed to have been inserted there by the parents of two small children who fell from a temporary bridge that replaced one destroyed in the Civil War. But M. Lovett Turner suggests that the figures are of adults and may have come from a chapel at Stoke-sub-Hamdon that was despoiled at that time.

A more romantic story with at least a germ of truth in it concerns Beggar's Bridge, a stone bridge over the River Esk, near Egton in Yorkshire. It was built by a man named Tom Ferris to keep a vow. As a young and impecunious man he had courted a girl called Agnes Richardson who lived on the other side of the river, which he crossed by stepping stones when the water was low but was unable to ford in times of flood. He promised to build a bridge there when he became rich. But riches seemed far off, and Agnes's father refused to let his daughter marry a 'beggar'. Tom eventually sailed from Whitby to fight against the Armada, and Agnes promised to leave a light shining in her bedroom window so that he could see she was still waiting for him when he returned, as she had always done whenever the river was impassable.

Tom did well at sea, collected a good deal of prize money, and returned to find the light still shining in Agnes's bedroom window. Her father withdrew his objection to the marriage and the couple apparently lived happily at Hull, where Tom became a wealthy merchant. He died there in 1631, as can be seen from his monument in the parish church, but not before he had kept his word and built the bridge which has stood since 1619.

Some 20 miles north of Hull at Harpham is a famous Drummer's Well, which contains the body of a drummer boy.

Page 71 (above) *The lonely Mermaid's Pool on the wild Morridge, Staffordshire;* (below) *Swarkestone Bridge, Derbyshire, stretches three-quarters of a mile across the Trent flood-plain*

Page 72 (above) *The Trent is said to claim three bodies annually;* (below) *the bells of Whitby Abbey, Yorkshire, can still be heard under the sea*

There are two versions of how he got there. One says he accidentally collided with the lord of the manor while playing the drum at an archery contest and fell into the well, an accident which prompted his mother to predict that he would be heard drumming whenever a member of the magnate's family was about to die. The other simply says that he was murdered and his body dumped into the well. Whatever the truth, it is said that the sound of drumming can sometimes be heard coming from the well.

The much-visited Silent Pool at Albury, just below Newland's Corner in Surrey, is also haunted, this time by the ghost of a lovely girl called Emma who chose to suffer a death worse than fate. She was bathing in the nude—usually safe enough in the days before tourism—when Prince (later King) John suddenly rode up with a band of equally lecherous henchmen. Emma, anxious to preserve her modesty and virginity, waded out of her depth, and, despite the efforts of her brother to rescue her, was drowned.

E

# CHAPTER
# SIX

# SAINTS AND MARTYRS

THERE are enough legends about British saints to fill several volumes rather than one short chapter. Cornwall is particularly rich in obscure Celtic saints, some of whom could occasionally stoop to most unsaintly conduct. St Just, for instance, is said to have slipped a silver wine cup into his baggage after a visit to his friend St Keverne, who lived near the Lizard. Soon discovering his loss, St Keverne set off in pursuit. Crossing Crowza Downs, he picked up some iron-stone boulders weighing several hundred pounds each and slipped them into his evidently capacious pockets. On catching sight of the retreating St Just, he hurled the stones at him. St Just thereupon threw away the cup and retreated more rapidly towards his home in West Penwith, leaving St Keverne to recover his property. The boulders, known as the Crowza Stones, remain where they fell to this day.

This was not St Just's only fall from grace. Another time he quarrelled so violently with a Sennen neighbour that they threw large lumps of granite at one another. Two of them, clashing in flight, merged into one enormous block, which has remained where it fell ever since.

Such conduct amongst the saints seems to have been comparatively rare, however. Most of them devoted their time to healing and other good deeds, though some were capable of violent action when required. The heart-shaped rock which is pointed out to visitors to St Michael's Mount was the heart of an unpleasant giant who occupied the Mount to the consternation of the local fishermen until St Michael—probably not the archangel—killed him in the year 495.

More often, though, it was the saint who suffered violence.
One notable victim was St Edmund, a ninth-century Saxon
king of East Anglia. After losing a battle against heathen
Viking raiders at Hoxne in the Waveney Valley, Edmund
hid from his pursuers under Goldbrook Bridge there. Unfortunately the reflection of his gilt spurs shining in the water
was seen by a newly married couple passing over the bridge.
They reported their find to the Danes, who captured him,
tied him to a nearby oak tree and riddled him with arrows.
Before his death, St Edmund laid a curse on all bridal
couples passing over the bridge, and it is said that newly-
weds still avoid its successor when returning from the marriage service. Local tradition also has it that the tree against
which he died survived until the turn of this century. It
seems to be true that an oak blown down about then had
several arrow heads buried in its trunk. Close to the site of
this tree is an old house known as Abbey Farm. It occupies
the site of an ancient wooden chapel where St Edmund's
bones rested for a while before their removal for reburial at
Bury St Edmunds in 903. There is also a St Edmund's Hall
in Hoxne that contains stirrups and other things possibly
connected with St Edmund that have been found in the
village or in the Goldbrook. The Abbey at Bury St Edmunds
became a noted place of pilgrimage until the Dissolution,
and its fine decorated gateway remains as another link with
this Christian martyr.

Violent death was also the fate of Earl Ethelwold, whose
story is told in slightly fading lettering on a stone cross called
Deadman's Plack in Harewood Forest south of Andover in
Hampshire. The monument dates only to 1835, but the story
goes back to about AD965. Ethelwold was certainly no saint,
not strictly a martyr, and his inclusion here can be justified
only by a link with St Edward the Martyr, and because I like
the story, though it is a sordid one of the type that would
nowadays hit the headlines in the popular Sunday press.

Ethelwold was a trusted earldorman of King Edgar, who, although under thirty, had already had two wives and was looking for a third. Having heard glowing accounts of the charms of Elfrida, daughter of Ordgar, Earl of Devonshire, he dispatched Ethelwold to Tavistock to meet the lady and give his expert opinion. Unfortunately, Ethelwold fell in love with Elfrida himself, and after sending back news to the king that her charms had been over-rated, he married her himself. But eventually Edgar became suspicious and he invited Ethelwold and his wife to court. Sensing the danger, Ethelwold tried to persuade his wife to put on her dowdiest clothes and dumbest manner, but Elfrida, having social ambitions, did precisely the opposite and scored a tremendous hit with the king, who promptly arranged to take Ethelwold hunting in a lonely part of Harewood Forest, and stabbed him with a javelin. Edgar then married the eager, merry widow, but died at the age of thirty-one, leaving Elfrida with a son Ethelred and a step-son Edward.

Being a scheming woman with a preference for her own son, she murdered Edward. According to one account she stabbed him. Another version is that she poisoned him with a drugged stirrup cup. The incident is supposed to have occurred at Corfe Castle, though in fact the present castle had not then been built, and occasionally the ghost of Edward is seen and heard riding over the bridge there, though that also had not been built at the time of the murder. Yet another story says that the body was taken to a blind woman's cottage at Corfe, covered over to hide his identity. The blind woman sat up all night with the body, and when the room was filled with a bright light from heaven she was able to see that this was the king. Eventually the body was taken to Shaftesbury Abbey for burial. The abbey became a place of pilgrimage and the memorial slab can still be seen. Several churches are dedicated to St Edward, King and Martyr, whose figure appears on the village sign at Corfe Castle and in church windows at Wareham and Salisbury Cathedral, among others. Elfrida, incidentally, retired from scheming and founded a nunnery at Wherwell in Hampshire, where she spent the rest of her life, though whether as a genuine act of penitence or as an insurance policy against the next world must be a matter of conjecture.

The young King Ethelbert of East Anglia also came to a violent end, being murdered on the instructions of Offa, king of Mercia, whom he was visiting at Sutton Walls, near Hereford. When various miracles occurred round Ethelbert's grave at Marden, Offa had the body moved to Hereford, and a well sprang up out of the empty grave. Miracles of healing continued to be performed by the new grave at Hereford, and the now repentant Offa had a magnificent shrine erected over it. Later, Hereford Cathedral was built on the site and dedicated jointly to St Ethelbert and the Virgin Mary. And at Marden the holy well can still be seen at the west end of the parish church.

One of Offa's successors as king of Mercia, Kenelm, son of King Kenulph, was himself murdered after dreaming of his own fate, as Chaucer's Nun's Priest reminds us. Kenelm was the victim of an ambitious elder sister, Quendryda, who hoped to become queen of Mercia. She persuaded a courtier named Askobert to take the boy hunting in the Clent Hills in Worcestershire, kill him, and bury him there. These instructions were carried out, and as no trace of the boy could be found, Quendryda eventually achieved her ambition. But her reign was brief. After the Pope, while celebrating Mass in St Peter's, Rome, received a message, borne in the beak of a dove, that

> In Clent, in Cowbach, lieth under a thorn
> His head off-shorn, Kenelm King-born,

he organised a search, and the body was found. It was reburied next to his father's grave at Winchcombe in Gloucestershire. Quendryda, though denying all knowledge of the crime, was driven from the country. St Kenelm's Church, Romsley, is believed to be built on the spot where the boy's body was found. It contains a modern window illustrating scenes from the legend, appropriately given in memory of child victims of World War 1, and a small statue on the outside of the south wall that may represent St Kenelm. The holy well that inevitably sprang up where the body was found is now under the boiler room of the church.

A better preserved holy well is St Winifrede's Well at Holywell in Flintshire. St Winifrede was the only child of a seventh-century local chief. She rejected the ardent advances of a Prince Caradog, who pursued her and was sufficiently frustrated as to cut off her head with his sword. The head rolled downhill and a spring of healing water emerged from the spot where it stopped. Her uncle, St Beunno, picked up the head and refitted it to her body, and she came to life with only a thin white ring to indicate the joint. She lived for a further fifteen years as abbess of Gwytherin in Denbighshire. St Winifrede's Well is still a landmark for tourists.

A similar story is told of St Osyth, after whom the village near Clacton on Sea is named. Her head was cut off by Viking raiders, but she tucked it under her arm and carried it a quarter of a mile to a church which stood in what is now called The Nun's Wood, where the usual healing well promptly gushed out of the ground.

Holy wells in fact are numerous in Britain. Many had the sort of curative powers which attracted visits from the sick and infirm as Lourdes does today. Several of these were linked with St Anne. The one at Buxton had a tradition of miraculous cures, and though it was closed for a time after the Reformation it has long been revived. It is now enclosed in a pavilion in the Crescent, where for a small charge you can drink a glass of the warmish healing water.

St Chad was another saint responsible for the appearance of various wells, mostly in the Midlands. The most famous can be seen at Stowe, near Lichfield. It was in this spring that St Chad stood naked as a penance, and by its side he built a small oratory on the site of what is now St Chad's Church, the city's oldest church. It was a noted place of pilgrimage in the Middle Ages, and thanks to the writing of a local doctor, Sir John Floyer, who recommended total immersion in it as a panacea, it became the centre of a flourishing spa in the early eighteenth century.

St Augustine's Well at Cerne Abbas in Dorset is another that can still be visited. The story here is that St Augustine, when he and his followers were tired and thirsty, thrust his pastoral staff into the dry ground, causing water to gush out, rather as St Joseph did at Glastonbury, and other saints elsewhere.

A slight variation of this story concerns St Milburga, founder of Wenlock Abbey. She ordered her horse to strike its hoof upon a rock. Immediately a spring emerged from the ground which has flowed ever since, and used to be thought capable of curing eye troubles. The spring is at Stoke St Milborough, north-east of Ludlow. Unfortunately the surround to the well has been covered with a thick slab of concrete, which has not improved its appearance, and the water is being used to augment the supply to a local reservoir.

Some healing wells were commercialised, bringing great profit to their custodians until competition became too keen. When faced with such competition, a man in charge of a healing well at Llandrillo-yn-Rhôs, near Colwyn Bay, had the brilliantly profitable idea of turning his well into a cursing well. On payment of a fee one could invoke curses on one's enemies. But the custodian's income did not stop there. He charged an additional fee to people to have a curse removed. Eventually, however, his little racket was stopped and the well destroyed, though a more orthodox holy well, St Trillo's Well, has survived in a small stone building close to the beach.

Another surviving well is the christening well dedicated to St Plegmund at Plemonstall in Cheshire on what was once an island surrounded by marshes. It is not far from the lonely church where the tomb of the saint, later to be Alfred the Great's tutor and Archbishop of Canterbury, can still be seen.

While St Trillo and St Plegmund built themselves hermitages by their holy wells, other saints were content to live in caves. One of these was St Robert of Knaresborough, a twelfth-century saint. Even the fiercest of bulls would allow him to place his arm round its neck. St Robert's Cave, by the Nidd at Knaresborough, better known as the place where the notorious eighteenth-century murderer Eugene Aram hid the body of his victim Daniel Clark, can still be visited.

One of our best known saints is St Swithun, largely because his story concerns our favourite topic—the weather. The legend of forty wet days to follow rain on St Swithun's Day probably arose from the removal of his body from his requested burial place outside the Minster at Winchester to a more pretentious tomb inside the Cathedral that was dedicated to him.

Meteorologists may have disproved the consequences of rain on 15 July, but the story of St Bega illustrates the foolishness of relying on English weather. She was an Irish princess who was shipwrecked on the coast of Cumberland after fleeing from a loveless marriage with a Norwegian prince. When she asked the local Lord of Egremont for permission to build a nunnery on the cliff, he disapprovingly told her that she could have as much land as was covered by snow on the following day, which happened to be midsummer's day. He was somewhat shaken next morning to find snow covering the ground for some 3 miles around. The nunnery now seems to have vanished like the snow, but St Bees Head and the village of St Bees, both named after St Bega, are worth a visit on their own account.

# CHAPTER SEVEN

# CHURCHES AND MONASTERIES

A MONG the most persistent of our legends is that of the church that could not be built on its chosen site. The story crops up all over the place. Indeed it is said to account for the place-name of Stowe-Nine-Churches in Northampton-shire, close to both the M1 and the A5. The tale runs that the local Saxon thane, inspired by a holy man he heard preaching in the open, agreed to allow a church to be built on his land at the foot of a hill. The foundations were dug, but next morning the workmen found that the trench had been filled in overnight. They cleared the trench and began to build the walls, but the following morning they discovered the stones piled up and the trench again filled in. Altogether eight attempts were made, with similar results. Finally a workman agreed to keep watch at night. Next morning he reported that a monster with a vaguely hog-like head had spent a busy night filling in the trench and piling up the stones. The builders agreed that this was a visitation from God or the devil (de-pending on which version you accept) and moved the stones up to the top of the hill, where they were permitted to build undisturbed. The church is dedicated to St Michael and All Angels—like so many hill-top churches—and contains some Saxon work, which at least confirms the rough date of the story.

It is odd about the monster's hog-like face, because it was pigs who selected the site of churches at Burnley and Win-wick in Lancashire, both of which have small effigies of pigs carved on the walls. In both cases, as at Stowe, the work com-pleted each day was demolished at night, but this pig did have the decency to cart the stones to the site he had chosen. When the workmen eventually accepted the inevitable, they were allowed to complete their task without further trouble, as indeed were the builders of another Lancashire church, at Leyland. This should have been erected at nearby Whittle, but a large, energetic and persistent cat dictated the final choice of site.

That the devil himself was responsible for moving the stones of the new church to a hill-top site, seems to have been accepted by the builders of Westwood Church, near Bradford-on-Avon, for his stone figure forms a corbel to the turret staircase there. There is less certainty, however, about the force behind the removal of Crosby Garrett Church in Westmorland from the village in the valley to the summit of the hill to the north.

There is an original twist to the story of the building of Christchurch Priory, though the first part follows the familiar pattern. The original site was on St Catherine's Hill, but each morning the materials had been moved about a mile to the south. As before, the builders accepted the new position and began to work unmolested. But here comes the new angle. An extremely enthusiastic workman joined the labour force, though he always seemed to miss meals and pay-times. When a beam proved to have been cut a foot short of its required length, he touched it and it immediately fitted into place. When the church was finished the workman simply vanished, but his colleagues, satisfied as to his identity, insisted that the church be called Christchurch. The beam, incidentally, is still in the church.

The craftsmanship of another remarkable workman can be seen in Roslyn Chapel, 8 miles south of Edinburgh. The whole of this small chapel—with its charnel house below—is outstandingly beautiful, but its most elaborate feature is the exquisite 'Prentice Pillar', wreathed in spirals of stone foliage. The familiar story is that it was the work of a young apprentice who carved the pillar during the absence of the master-mason. On his return the mason was so enraged with jealousy at being outdone by his apprentice that he killed the lad with a hammer. Another story of Roslyn Chapel, founded by William Sinclair—later Earl of Caithness—in 1446, is that whenever a member of the family is about to die the chapel appears to be on fire.

A much less beautiful piece of craftsmanship than that at Roslyn is the stump of the unfinished spire on the tower of Beeby Church in Leicestershire. The local explanation for this architectural monstrosity—known as 'Beeby Tub'—is that the Abbot of Croyland (or Crowland), who owned the church, intended to build a spire as fine as that at neighbour-ing Queniborough, and ordered two masons, brothers, who had done the spire there, to set to work at Beeby. There were difficulties from the start. Money was short and the two brothers disagreed over the plans. However, the work was started and went fairly well for about two months until the workmen struck over a delay in paying their wages. Either because of this or because of continued disagreement over the final appearance of the spire, the brothers quarrelled violently while they were working at a considerable height. They came to blows and both fell to the ground and were killed. Though the abbot eventually cleared up the arrears in wages, the spire was left unfinished.

So, for three centuries, was the spire of Porlock Church in Somerset, after it had been damaged in a gale. Its top is said to have been blown across country to settle on the roof of Culbone Church, a mile away. There is another story, told by M. Lovett Turner, that the builders repairing Porlock spire abandoned their work to join in a stag-hunt, and never bothered to return.

While on the subject of spires and towers, mention must be made of the curious creature that is represented in the iron weather-vane of St Mary's Church, Kingsclere in Hampshire.

Local opinion inclines to the view that it is a bed-bug, put there on the instructions of King John after a sleepless night in a lice-infested bed in a local inn.

Church windows tell their stories too, as we have already seen. One at St Mary's, Lambeth, commemorates the story of a pedlar whose dog dug up a box of gold coins in the fifteenth century when Lambeth was still rural. The pedlar replaced the soil, bought the land cheaply, and became rich on the proceeds of his find. He gave generously to the church on condition that he and his dog should be depicted in a stained-glass window. This was done, and though the window was destroyed in a 1941 blitz, it has been replaced by a modern one which not only displays the pedlar and his dog but also the London County Hall, which was built on the site of the original 'pedlar's acre'.

A rather similar story is told of another pedlar, John Chapman, who certainly paid for the north aisle and tower of the magnificent church at Swaffham in Norfolk. He struck it rich after dreaming that if he went to London and stood on London Bridge he would 'hear something to his advantage'. So off he went to London Bridge, where he hung about for some time before telling his story to a local shopkeeper who scornfully told him not to be so silly. The shopkeeper said that he had had a similar dream about a pot of gold hidden under a tree in the back garden of a pedlar named John Chapman at Swaffham in Norfolk, but like Chaucer's Pertelôte he had no faith in dreams. At this news, Chapman, without revealing his name, hurried back home, dug under his tree, and found not only a pot of gold but an inscription on the lid of the pot advising him, in Latin, to dig deeper. This he did and found another pot containing twice as much gold. You can still see two carvings of Chapman, one with his wife and another with his dog, in the church that he so richly endowed, and his story is also commemorated in the splendid modern name-board at the approaches to this pleasant little market town.

Variations of the Chapman story, starting with the dream and the visit to London Bridge, are told in Wales and also at Upsall, in the Hambledon Hills in Yorkshire, but there is no tradition that the pedlars made any gifts to local churches.

However, there are some curious stories about the founding of churches in different parts of the country. The lonely church 1,000ft up on the summit of Brent Tor in Devon is said to have been erected by a sea-captain who avoided grounding his ship by a glimpse of the Tor, from which he got a bearing just in time. He built the church as a thank-offering. Two churches at Stocklinch in Somerset were reputedly built by two sisters in a spirit of rivalry, and a similar story accounts for the two churches at Bywell in Northumberland, while the two churches sharing a single churchyard at Willingale Spain and Willingale Doe in Essex are supposed to have been built by rival knights.

Of haunted churches, the most famous is undoubtedly the chapel of St Peter-ad-Vincula in the Tower of London. The story has often been told of a sentry who saw a light in the chapel one night and sent for an officer. The two fetched a ladder, climbed it, and saw a procession of people in Tudor dress walking up and down inside, led by a figure which was undoubtedly Anne Boleyn. After a short time the figures vanished and so did the light. Anne is supposed to be buried in the chapel, but tradition says that her body was later removed, either to Salle in Kent or Horndon-on-the-Hill in Essex. A black marble slab at Salle that was supposed to cover her tomb was eventually moved, revealing an empty grave, but the Horndon story may well be true.

Another haunted London church is St Bartholomew-the-Great, Smithfield, where the footsteps of the founder, Rahere, Henry I's jester, are said to be heard pacing up and down the aisles and ambulatories. Ghostly footsteps are also heard at night in the church at Hinckley in Leicestershire. They are reputedly those of a monk.

Page 89 *Two holy wells: (above) St Chad's Well, Stowe, Staffordshire; (below) St Augustine's Well, Cerne Abbas, Dorset*

SWAFFHAM

Ye Pedlar of Swaffham
who did by a dream
find a great treasure

(left) *This delightful village sign at Swaffham, Norfolk, illustrates the story of a pedlar who found a fortune;* (below) *the 'Tub' at Beeby, Leicestershire*

Most haunted churches are of monastic foundation. Monks are heard faintly singing vespers on summer evenings in the parish church of Beaulieu, which is built on the site of the abbey refectory. A cowled monk was seen at Battle Abbey when the church was damaged by fire in 1931, and he reappeared in the following year.

Many monastic sites became private houses after the Dissolution, and the ghosts who still haunt these will be mentioned in a later chapter, but this might be an appropriate place to deal with the ghost of ruined Guisborough Priory in Yorkshire. He is a monk in a black habit who is said to turn out on the night of the first new moon of every year to check that the treasure buried by the Augustinian canons has not been disturbed. According to Michael Parkin about a hundred ghost-hunters turned out to await the arrival of the black monk in 1966 and 1967. Some visitors reported seeing a cowled figure in 1966, but the next year's apparition was undoubtedly a hoaxer. In 1968, when only a few spectators turned out in the cold, nothing at all was seen.

Although many people are fearful of passing graveyards at night, I know of few stories of hauntings on consecrated ground. But there is a curious and undoubtedly true story of the grave of William Davies in the churchyard at Montgomery. Davies was hanged in November 1821, during a thunderstorm, for the crime of highway robbery with violence, although he was almost certainly innocent. Before his execution he predicted that no grass would grow over his grave for a generation—and he was proved right. Various attempts were made later in the century to re-seed the ground, and new turf was introduced without much success. To this day a small cross of sterile ground remains over his grave.

F

# CHAPTER EIGHT

# STATELY GHOSTS AND LEGENDS

THE ghosts that haunt Britain's stately homes are 'rapidly dwindling', according to James Lees-Milne, partly through the installation of electricity but mainly because of 'the constant shuffling of tourists' feet'. Basically, it is true that some of our most celebrated ghosts have been relatively inactive over the last few decades, but occasionally one pops out to confound Mr Lees-Milne, and many of our ancient castles and stately homes wear an aura that suggests that they are still bristling with ghosts.

Glamis, ancestral home of the Earl of Strathmore and birthplace of Princess Margaret, is perhaps the classic example. In addition to its hundred or so rooms, there is supposed to be a secret chamber in which a much earlier earl kept hidden a son who was half human, half monster. This strange creature is said to have lived there for 150 years, emerging only at night, and the whereabouts of the hidden chamber was a secret passed on only by each earl to his heir. Nearly a century ago the members of a house party took advantage of their host's temporary absence to search for the room. They hung out towels from every window in the castle. Then they went round the outside of the building and found seven windows from which no towel hung. Unfortunately, the return of the earl put a stop to further exploration.

*Lord Halifax's Ghost Book* contains various detailed eyewitness accounts from the last century of strange things seen and heard at Glamis, including the figure of a giant—perhaps the monster from the secret chamber. Other Glamis ghosts include that of Earl Baerdie, who is reputed to have to play cards eternally, having lost his soul to the devil in a card game, and Jane Douglas, who was burnt as a witch in the sixteenth century for her alleged part in an attempt to murder King James V.

Windsor Castle is comparatively peaceful after Glamis, but the ghost of Elizabeth I has occasionally been seen in the library there. Royal ghosts make more frequent appearances at Hampton Court Palace, especially in the 'Haunted Gallery', where the unhappy spirit of Catherine Howard has often been seen and heard. Her story is that when she was arrested on the instructions of her husband, Henry VIII, she eluded her guards and dashed down the gallery towards the chapel where the king was at prayer. Her attempt to plead with him was thwarted by a guard at the chapel door. Her screams as she was led away have echoed down the centuries and are said to have been heard by reputable witnesses in recent times. Occasionally she has been seen, dressed in white like another of Henry's queens, Jane Seymour, who reputedly comes from the queen's apartments carrying a lighted taper, glides along the Silver Stick Gallery and then disappears down the stairs.

Yet another ghost of Hampton Court Palace is that of Mistress Sibell Penn, Edward VI's dearly-loved nurse, whose story is described in some detail by Christina Hole. Her ghost did not trouble the palace until her monument was removed from Hampton Church in 1829. After that she was seen several times wandering around her old rooms in the palace, and occasionally the sound of a spinning-wheel could be heard in that direction. During later alterations a forgotten room was found, containing a spinning-wheel that may have belonged to Mistress Penn. According to Miss Hole, footsteps are still heard from time to time in the old rooms, and the ghost of Mistress Penn has been seen by people in the palace in recent years.

Most royal ghosts seem to be connected with the Tudors.

Catherine of Aragon is reputed to appear occasionally in the gallery at Kimbolton Castle, Huntingdonshire, while Mary Tudor haunts Sawston Hall, near Cambridge, always wearing the dress that appears in her portrait that hangs in the Great Hall there, and always carrying a prayer book. It is in the Tapestry Room that her ghost appears, and it is said that no one can sleep there in peace. It was in that room that Mary spent one night in 1553 shortly before she became queen, taking refuge from the Duke of Northumberland who planned to imprison her and put Lady Jane Grey on the throne. Mary's night there was brief. Early in the morning she was warned that Northumberland's men were near. Disguised as a milkmaid, she slipped off just in time. Northumberland's men, in their rage, set fire to Sawston Hall, but Mary promised that when she reigned she would build a better house for her Roman Catholic friends, the Huddlestons. She kept her word. The new house—incorporating part of the earlier one, including the Tapestry Room—was completed in 1584, and is still there; still occupied at the time of writing by the Huddlestons—and, it is said, by the ghost of Mary Tudor.

One of Mary's enemies, Henry Grey, Duke of Suffolk, beheaded on Tower Hill for his part in the revolt against her, haunts Astley Castle in Warwickshire. The castle, actually a moated, fortified manor house, was pulled down after Suffolk's execution, but was soon rebuilt to incorporate what remained of the earlier house. The headless duke is still said to haunt the place, which is now a hotel.

One would expect the unhappy spirit of that other Mary, Queen of Scots, to haunt the numerous houses where she was held captive, but, so far as I know, Lyme Hall in Cheshire is the only haunted house linked with her. Even there, though the room she occupied is the haunted one, it is probably not her ghost that appears in it. It seems to be the spirit of the unknown person whose skeleton was found under the floor of a secret chamber who wanders around the place, accompanied occasionally by the ringing of distant bells. The usual theory is that it is the ghost of a Jesuit priest, but some young friends of mine who attended a youth conference there are convinced that they saw the figure of a woman wandering around the house.

Other royal ghosts make spasmodic appearances. George III is seen at times at Kensington Palace. The heavy footsteps heard clattering around Forde House, Newton Abbot, are said to be those of William III who slept there on his first night in England after landing at Brixham. The Black Prince, in armour, turns up around dusk at Hall Place, Bexley, whenever danger threatens the occupants or the nation. He is said to have been seen several times before British defeats in the two world wars.

Similarly, Drake's Drum is said to roll unaided when England is in danger, as a signal that its original owner is prepared to return, in Arthurian style, to drum the enemy up the Channel. It is supposed to have been heard during World War 1, and in the ships at Scapa Flow when the German Grand Fleet came to anchor there before they were scuttled. This, the oldest English drum extant, was restored to Buckland Abbey in 1968 in part payment of estate duties after spending four years in the vaults of a London bank, where it apparently remained silent through a financial crisis which even Drake felt himself unable to resolve.

Berry Pomeroy Castle, also in Devon, used to be haunted by the ghost of a young woman who appeared when any of the family there were about to die. She was reputedly a Pomeroy who had a child by her own father. Now that the castle is ruined she must be redundant, but the tradition that the place is haunted persists.

So it does at Goodrich Castle, beautifully situated on the Wye. This was the last Herefordshire stronghold to fight for Charles I, and it is haunted by the ghosts of Alice Birch and Charles Clifford, who were drowned in the river while

attempting to escape when the castle finally fell to Colonel
Birch's attack.

Castles tend to be haunted by females rather than males.
Rochester Castle has had a White Lady wandering through
the building for more than 800 years, and another Kentish
castle, Chiddingstone, has an equestrian lady ghost, thought
to be a member of the Streatfield family whose manor house
this was for many generations. Blenkinsopp Castle in Northumberland has its own White Lady. She is the ghost of a
Lady de Blenkinsopp, who was married by the castle's owner
for her wealth. Unfortunately for him, she was careful with
her money and hid it in a treasure chest within the castle
precincts, wisely refusing to disclose its whereabouts to her
husband, who eventually took umbrage and walked out on
her. After a while, she set out in search of him, but neither
returned alive, though her ghost, dressed in white, has been
seen often since, searching the castle either for her husband
or for the treasure chest whose whereabouts seems to have
slipped her memory.

There are male ghosts as well. Hurstmonceaux Castle has
a giant phantom drummer who is reputed to beat his drum
on the battlements at times, though he seems to have been
strangely subdued since the arrival of the scientists of the
Royal Observatory, who also appear to have successfully
driven off the numerous other ghosts who were supposed to
haunt the place.

Nor have there been recent reports of the appearance of
the 'Cauld Lad' of Hylton, who haunts Hylton Castle, near
Sunderland, a ruin now cared for by the Department of the
Environment. He was a groom who was killed by his master,
Robert Hylton, in a moment of frenzy in 1609. Hylton hid
the body under some straw and later threw it into a pond,
where the skeleton was found many years later. But the lad
continued to haunt the castle, apparently with his head in
his hands, according to Peter A. White, creating a great deal

of noise in the murder room right up to the time the building was last inhabited in 1905.

One would expect this northern border country, with its tradition of violence, to be fruitful in ghosts, and so it is. Vanbrugh's Seaton Delavel Hall has a famous Grey Lady (or White Lady—there seems to be doubt about the colour of her dress) who survived the savage fire of 1822 to keep watch at one of the windows, apparently awaiting the return of her lover. Bellister Castle, another Blenkinsopp seat, has a Grey Man ghost. He was a wandering minstrel who was given hospitality by the reigning owner but later aroused unwarranted suspicions that he was a spy sent by an unfriendly neighbour. When the minstrel left, bloodhounds were sent after him. They caught him up and tore him to pieces on the banks of the Tyne, since when the ghost of this unjustly suspected man has haunted the castle.

Haughton Castle, which stands superbly above the Tyne, is haunted by the ghost of a certain Archie Armstrong, who was thrown into a dungeon on suspicion of some crime. It was only intended to keep him there overnight, but when the owner was suddenly called away, poor Archie was forgotten and left to die of starvation.

This story reminds me of the better known one of Lady Elizabeth Hoby of Bisham Abbey, who died there in 1609 aged ninety-one and was buried in the tomb which she designed herself and that can still be seen in Bisham Church on the banks of the Thames near Marlow. Lady Hoby was an intellectual with an almost modern neurosis about the education of her children, and one of her sons who was less bright than the rest was constantly beaten for bad work. One day she locked him in a room to finish some work as a punishment, and being hurriedly summoned to Queen Elizabeth's court, she left without remembering to tell the servants about her son. He was dead when she eventually returned, his head resting on a tear-stained book. It is said that she never forgave herself for her neglect—or for her cruelty, for another version rejects the locked room story and simply says that she beat the boy to death in a fit of rage.

There are curious features about the whole tale. One is the absence of any mention of a William Hoby among the four children on her monument or in the family pedigree, leading to a belief that the whole thing was a myth. But when alterations were being made to the abbey in 1840, some old copybooks turned up behind a skirting board. One of them was badly blotted. These books have since disappeared, but Lady Hoby has not, it seems. She appeared to Admiral Vansittart, a more recent occupant of the abbey. She has even been photographed, though a photograph may be faked. But even since 1946, while Bisham Abbey has belonged to the Central Council of Physical Recreation, loud weeping has been heard at night and footsteps have been heard walking along a non-existent corridor.

Another much-haunted abbey is Newstead, Byron's old home, which has almost as many ghosts as Glamis. The most famous is the Black Friar, whose appearance heralded disaster to some member of the Byron family. The poet said he saw the friar shortly before his marriage to Anne Milbanke, but this may have been a typically cynical remark. However, there is a tradition that a few days before the poet's death, the friar was seen by a servant. This girl had slipped out to meet her boy-friend in the cloisters, but met the Black Friar instead—and promptly fainted. The poor girl was perhaps lucky that she did not meet the 'shapeless black mass with glaring eyes' that also haunted the cloisters, perhaps not the most attractive spot for an evening date.

The cloisters were not commonly visited by the Black Friar, who seems to have been more at home in the so-called Haunted Chamber, where he terrified more than one sceptical guest by appearing from a cupboard, leering unpleasantly at the room's occupant, and then vanishing. Such visits were usually followed by a death in the Byron family.

The Black Friar was also reputed to appear whenever the abbey changed hands, but so far as I know, he was not seen when the city of Nottingham acquired the property. Nor, I believe, have any of the other ghosts, such as the headless monk, or 'Little Sir John with the Great Beard', a studious spirit who used to sit below his portrait in the library reading a book. The phantom horsemen who were sometimes heard riding in the park at night seem to have been silent in recent years, and the garden roller is no longer pushed along gravel paths at times when it was thought to be securely locked away, as happened several times when Colonel Wildman lived at the abbey after the Byrons. In his day any servant who even mentioned a ghost was instantly sacked, but today it seems that the Newstead ghosts disapprove of municipal ownership, and even an impending rise in local taxes fails to bring out the Black Friar or his associates.

Michelham Priory in Sussex, on the other hand, has suddenly become more haunted than ever. Its gatehouse has for long been rather nebulously troubled by a Grey Lady, who seems only to have been seen by friends of people who had friends who had heard of her being seen. But in the summer of 1967 my brother Garth, who was President of the Friends of the Priory until his sudden death later that year, told me of the appearance of at least two new ghosts. The local press then got hold of the story, which was featured in an article by James Donne in *Sussex Life* for December 1967.

In July of that year, three visitors from Seaford were admiring the great fireplace in the large Tudor Room when a tall figure wearing the habit of the Augustine canons who built the priory in 1229 'walked clean through the wall and appeared to walk down some stairs that were not there, crossed to the far end of the room, turned round and walked out of the open door into the Priory'. Only two of the visitors saw this apparition, but all three, less than a minute later, not only saw, but stepped out of the way of, a 'lady wearing a bluish-grey gown' who entered the room, 'crossed it and went into the little room adjoining, where she completely disappeared, apparently through the outer stone wall of the priory'. Her dress was described as 'of early Tudor or medieval style'. The time was around three in the afternoon, an unusual hour for a ghostly visitation.

A friend of mine, a phlegmatic collier not given to flights of imagination, had a somewhat similar experience a few years earlier in the crumbling shell of Codnor Castle, overlooking D. H. Lawrence's Erewash Valley. In broad daylight he watched a Cromwellian soldier cross the courtyard and vanish through an arch. The miner's dog saw him too, for 'his hair fairly bristled', my friend told me later in a radio interview. A thorough and immediate search proved the precincts to be deserted. The odd thing here is that there is no tradition of previous hauntings, and the only link with the Civil War is that the castle was despoiled afterwards, like so many other potential Royalist strongholds.

An older established ghost is that of 'Wild' Will Darrell of Littlecote in Wiltshire, for John Aubrey recounted the story in the seventeenth century and it was later used by Sir Walter Scott—with suitable embellishments—in *Rokeby*. Briefly, the story is that in the reign of Queen Elizabeth I, Will Darrell, then owner of Littlecote, sent our hurriedly for a midwife, a Mrs Barnes from the village of Great Shefford over the Berkshire border. She was told to attend a Lady Knyvett immediately, but that she had to travel blindfolded. Somewhat reluctantly, after being promised a fat fee, she accepted, and was driven hurriedly to a mansion which she did not recognise when the handkerchief was removed from her eyes, but which has always been presumed to be Littlecote.

There the baby was duly delivered, the mother being masked so that Mrs Barnes could not identify her. Immediately afterwards, a man, assumed to be 'Wild' Will Darrell, dashed into the room, seized the baby, carried it into another room and threw it on to a blazing fire, which he stirred with his boot until no trace of the body remained.

Mrs Barnes later told her story to a cousin of Darrell's, who some time afterwards wrote it down from memory. Who the mother was is doubtful. Lady Knyvett, Ada Darrell, Will's sister, and a girl named Bonham who was supposed to be his mistress, have all been suggested. Sir Henry Knyvett suspected it was his wife's child, but Christopher Hussey has suggested that the whole story may have been fabricated to 'frame' Darrell, who seems to have been extremly unpopular with neighbours and tenants.

However, the screams of mother, midwife and baby are said to be heard in the night at Littlecote, and 'Wild' Will's ghost is believed to haunt the house and a lane nearby. Visitors to Littlecote are shown a fireplace on a landing in which the baby is said to have been thrown, and the haunted room leading off the landing.

Another much haunted house is Raynham Hall in Norfolk. Its most famous ghost is the 'Brown Lady', who was Dorothy Walpole, Sir Robert's sister. She married the second Viscount Townshend, who soon tired of her charm, became irritated by her extravagance, and finally refused to allow her access to her own children. It is possibly in search of them that she wanders down the main staircase and along various passages.

She has been seen many times. A Major Loftus, who saw her twice when he visited Raynham in 1849, reported that she had sockets instead of eyes. After this (according to the Marchioness Townshend of Raynham), the servants gave notice, and detectives were engaged among the new staff without being able to lay the ghost. Captain Marryat, the novelist, saw her, and afterwards slept with pistols under his pillow. On a second sighting he is reputed to have fired at her. The bullet went through her, it is said, and was found next morning embedded in the door. There have been more recent visits, and a *Country Life* photographer obtained a remarkable picture of the ghost on the stairs.

Dorothy Walpole also haunts nearby Houghton Hall, where she spent a much happier part of her life. There is a story that she appeared to the Prince Regent in the State Bedroom, and though he was not normally unhappy about nocturnal visits from ladies, he was so disturbed by the Brown Lady that he asked to sleep in another room on the following night.

But let us return to Raynham, where there are other ghosts. The famous Duke of Monmouth haunts the room in which he once slept and which is named after him. The Marchioness Townshend reported that an elderly spinster found a visit from his ghost an agreeable and flattering experience. And the marchioness also claimed that two ghost children and a spectral spaniel haunt the house. Strange noises are heard in the picture gallery and on the landing outside, and furniture is moved in the royal bedroom at night.

An equally troubled house is Sandford Orcas Manor, a charming Tudor residence hidden among deep Dorset lanes north of Sherborne, where the only vestige of rush-hour traffic is caused by cows heading for the milking sheds at four in the afternoon. When my wife and I visited the house in August 1967, I casually remarked to Mrs Claridge that I was interested in the ghost that haunted her home, to which she asked, equally casually, 'Which one? We have seven.'

The noisiest of these is a male ghost who haunts what is now the nursery wing. Sometimes he is seen; at others he just knocks on a door and then appears to drag a heavy body along a landing. Other ghosts reported by Denis Frost in an interview with Colonel Claridge, who occupies the house with his wife, include 'a white-haired old lady in a hand-painted red dress (a dress actually in the house, though locked in a cupboard), another lady in a high-necked Elizabethan gown, a man who once followed two members of the public seeing over the house...and a father who owned the manor...and hanged himself from a pulley set into the entrance arch'. All these have been seen in recent years. The man who committed suicide has been photographed, though imperfectly. Most of these ghostly visitations seem to have been concentrated in the nursery wing or the solar.

The Sandford Orcas ghosts attracted much publicity in 1966 and 1967. The journalists who descended on the house then saw and heard nothing, execpt that one party claimed to have seen an apparition outside the kitchen window just after Christmas in 1966. A team from the Paraphysical Laboratory at Downton conducted a very thorough investigation, whose results were summarised in the *Journal of Paraphysics* for 1967. They found five verifiable cases of apparitions or strange noises being seen or heard by people quite independent of the Claridge family between 1906 and 1966, though they admit that one of the five—the radio team—might have misinterpreted their experience 'through expectation or suggestion'. However, there were other independent reports which they did not include because the investigators, 'owing to various difficulties', had been 'unable to obtain corroborative data'. They concluded with a restrained verdict that 'a reasonable *prima facie* case had been made out for the hauntings'.

Athelhampton Manor, in the same county, possesses a more modest total of five ghosts including, rather unconventionally, that of a pet monkey belonging to the Martyn family who owned the house up to 1595. The ghostly monkey has not been seen for many years, but at least two members of the domestic staff have seen the Grey Lady of Athelhampton in recent years. Their experiences are recounted by J. Wentworth Day. A housemaid, now retired, told how the Grey Lady, assumed at first glance to be a visitor looking round the house, vanished through the wainscot when asked to leave. When confronted, more recently, by the housekeeper, the Lady in Grey, who had been sitting comfortably in the Tudor room, just faded away. One of the maids saw another ghost, called the Black Priest, outside a bathroom door in broad daylight. This hooded figure is presumably also left over from the Martyn occupation, for they were Roman Catholics and doubtless had their own priest. Another Athel-hampton ghost is a cooper who hammers away at wine barrels in the cellar, and for good measure a couple of young men occasionally refight a duel in the great chamber.

Page 107 (above) *Astley Castle, Warwickshire, is haunted by a Tudor Duke of Suffolk;* (below) *Beaulieu Church, Hampshire, where monks still sing in the ruined refectory*

Page 108 (above) *Remote Tunstead Farm, Derbyshire, the scene of a sinister story;* (below) *Rochester Castle, Kent, has had a White Lady wandering around for 800 years*

# CHAPTER
# NINE

# SCREAMING SKULLS
# AND OTHER ODDITIES

NOT all ghosts take the conventional form of brown, white or grey ladies or their masculine counterparts, with or without heads. That lovely, lofty mansion of Burton Agnes in the East Riding of Yorkshire is haunted by a screaming skull. It is the skull of Anne Griffiths, one of the three daughters and co-heiresses of Sir Henry Griffiths. After their father's death his daughters decided to rebuild the old house in the style of the period, about 1590, though the mansion was apparently not completed until the 1620s. Anne was particularly devoted to the new house. Unfortunately, shortly after it was finished she was brutally attacked and robbed in the road about a mile from the house and died from her injuries a few days later. Before dying she made her sisters promise to keep her head in the house, saying that otherwise she would make the place untenable.

But the surviving sisters had second thoughts and decided that a normal burial would be more seemly. They soon had cause to regret their decision. There followed a period of chaotic nights; of crashings and bangings, moanings and groanings that 'murdered sleep'. On the vicar's advice, the grave was reopened and the head—said to be already detached from the body—restored to the house.

Its return promptly put a stop to the noises, but they have restarted when any attempt has been made to bury or throw out the skull. There is a well-known tale of a newly arrived maid who, not knowing the story, found the skull and threw it on to a passing manure cart. The horse would not move another step, and after a brief commotion the skull was returned to the house. It is now bricked into one of the walls, though nobody is sure exactly where. The ghost of a small, thin woman in a fawn dress is occasionally seen about the house. She is apparently Anne Griffiths, and the story of her appearance in 1915 to the then owner, Mrs Wickham Boynton, is briefly told in *Lord Halifax's Ghost Book*.

There are several other houses that have skulls bricked into their walls—or have had—including Wardley Hall, near Manchester, home of the Bishop of Salford, and Bettiscombe Manor House, just north of the fascinating Marshwood Vale in west Dorset, where the top of the skull of a negro servant has rested since the eighteenth century. In these, and other places, attempts to remove the skulls have led to odd and often disastrous happenings.

My own favourite skull story is that of Dickie of Tunstead in my native Derbyshire. There are two Tunsteads in the county; this particular one is a hamlet in the extreme north-west between Whaley Bridge and Chapel-en-le-Frith. Oddly enough, nobody knows whose skull it is, nor when it first found a resting place in the sombre, remote, north-facing Tunstead Farm, or whether it is still there. The present occupants, naturally perhaps, are reticent on the subject. Nobody even knows Dickie's sex. The stories of a woman's ghost having been seen occasionally around the house suggest that it may be the skull of a female who was murdered there many years ago.

For years, Dickie successfully guarded the house, making noises on the approach of a stranger, was once instrumental by his bangings in having a burglar caught, and has survived immersion in a river and burial in the churchyard at Chapel-en-le-Frith, though locally it is believed that he has again been buried. Dickie's greatest triumphs, however, have been to get his name on to an Ordnance Survey map and to divert a railway.

The railway story relates to the building of the London

and North Western line from Buxton to Stockport. The engineers wanted to carry the line across a field belonging to Tunstead Farm. When the farmer objected, the company obtained compulsory powers. Then Dickie took a hand by organising a series of landslides. Eventually the line had to be diverted away from the farm, because, said the engineers, of 'the unstable nature of the ground'. But the locals knew the real cause. And a bridge across the line is officially designated 'Dickie's Bridge'.

Tunstead Farm is not a stately home in the accepted sense, and it is a common fallacy that 'things go bump in the night' only in vast mansions. Parsonages have their ghosts too. The Old Vicarage, Grantchester, is the classic example. Ever since Rupert Brooke's death in 1915 there have been stories of his footsteps being heard approaching the french window of the sitting-room from the outside. But the owner, Mr Peter Ward, a former Olympic runner, told me that, 'though our home is pretty full of manifestations of all kinds, all of them pleasant and harmless, none of them appears to be connected in any way with Rupert Brooke but with earlier happenings in the house'. He goes on to add that 'Having lived with them for fifty years I now take our ghosts for granted and live very much at peace with them'.

I do not know if Newark vicarage is still haunted, but I remember sometime in the 1930s the then vicar telling my father how, on returning home one morning, he saw the figure of a monk standing in front of his study fireplace. He hurried into the room by its only entrance, and found it empty. His wife assured him that no monk, or any other visitor, had called that morning.

Two vicarages in the Southwark diocese have recently been exorcised by Canon J. D. Pearce-Higgins, Vice-Provost of Southwark Cathedral, who was reported in *The Times* of 4 April 1968, as having 'cleared' ten houses of spirits in the previous eighteen months, mostly quite 'unstately' homes.

Curiously enough, the former Exorcist's House, adjoining
the churchyard of St Nicholas, King's Lynn, is itself haunted,
though 'not very enthusiastically', according to my friend Mr
F. R. Buckley, a well-known broadcaster, who lives in the
house.

Another literary friend, Mr Walter Brierley, had an odd
experience when he was courting his wife. She lived in a
smallish Georgian house called 'The Ridgeway' on the outskirts of the Derbyshire village of Heage. The house was
built by an ex-butler at Heage Hall, reputedly out of the
proceeds of money stolen over a period of years from his
master, a relative of Florence Nightingale.

Walter visited the house one cold Easter Monday to take
his girl-friend for a walk. She called downstairs that she was
nearly ready. Almost immediately afterwards the figure of a
young woman wearing a flimsy dress appeared at the top of
a dark staircase. 'Surely, you're not going out dressed like
that,' said Walter, 'you'll freeze to death.' There was no reply.
The figure descended the stairs, walked silently past him,
and vanished. A moment later Walter's future wife appeared
at the top of the stairs dressed for walking. 'A trick of the
light, I suppose,' says Walter, a little doubtfully.

It may be 'the shuffling of tourists' feet' or just the social
revolution of post-war years that has caused ghosts to haunt
more modest houses, but certainly many are not too proud to
move into council houses. Mr and Mrs Tucker and their
family had to be moved by the Swindon council in 1966 because their house, built only two years earlier, was haunted
by 'inexplicable noises, shadowy shapes, mysterious lights
and a sinister atmosphere'. The twenty-two-year-old son,
Victor, had even been grabbed by mysterious hands on the
landing. Another family had to leave their council house in
Newton Grove, Grimsby, in October 1967, after electric light
switches and gas taps had been mysteriously turned on and
off and clothes and furniture moved for no apparent reason.

A psychic expert who was called in reported that the house, built on the site of an old burial ground, was haunted by 'a hideous old man in a white habit'.

In February 1968 Nottingham Corporation was investigating an apparition which had made several appearances—occasionally breaking into song—in a council house in Denewood Crescent on the Clifton Estate, and since then a Roman Catholic priest has been called in by the urban council at Newton-le-Willows in Lancashire to bless a house in which a series of tenants have been bothered by a ghost. In 1968, *The Guardian* reported that a ghost over 6ft tall was troubling Mr and Mrs Peter Smith in their council house in Darlington Grove, Moorends, near Doncaster, even after the local vicar had been called in to say prayers in the house at 2.30 in the morning.

Many pubs are haunted, and I know one small hotel that takes its name from a ghost. This is The Lady in Grey at Shardlow in Derbyshire, a stone's throw from the Trent. Until fairly recently the hotel was a private house, dating from the eighteenth century, which belonged for many years to the Soresby family. The last Soresbys to live there were two maiden ladies who were devoted to the house, and it is one of them, dressed in Victorian clothes, who is supposed to haunt the house.

A later occupant, a business man with no taste for the occult, saw the ghostly lady cross the landing upstairs and enter his bedroom. Thinking it was his housekeeper, he called out to her, but she replied from downstairs and was certainly not wearing a Victorian grey dress. A thorough search of the house revealed nobody hidden away. Since then several people claim to have seen the phantom lady in grey and to have heard strange noises. The wife of the present proprietor tells me that she has twice felt somebody brush past her in the garden but has seen nobody.

The head waiter of the same hotel had not seen that ghost,

but told me that when he was working at the Friary Hotel in Derby, built on the site of a house of the Blackfriars, he was passed in the corridor by a black friar. Until then he had always laughed when other waiters and guests had reported seeing a black friar in the same corridor.

The ancient Crown Hotel at Alton in Hampshire has at least two ghosts that are still active. One is the ghost of a dog that was beaten to death by a drunken customer, who threw the remains on the fire. When the brewers, during an extensive restoration in 1967, pulled out three old fireplaces they found a quantity of animal bones. Mr Ray Curtis, then the licensee, told an *Alton Herald* reporter that his two pet dogs 'whenever they go into that room start howling, and scratching at the fireplace'. The second ghost is a White Lady, thought to be a kitchen maid who was murdered in the Crown. She moves around the hotel at night. 'When we first came to the place, we often heard footsteps in the passageway upstairs by our bedroom,' Mr Curtis said. 'We're convinced that there's something there.' Neither the restoration nor a change of licensee disturbed the White Lady, it seems, for Mrs R. McNeil, the present licensee's wife, swears that someone enters the old bar every night after she has locked up and moves the position of a lampshade, while one of her children is frightened to enter the bathroom because, she says, she has seen a White Lady there.

The Red Lion, facing the spacious green across the Roman Stane Street at Ockley in Surrey, has a low, oak-beamed bedroom that is supposed to be haunted by the ghost of a young lady who was brought there dying after a hunting accident many years ago. I must say that I spent two comfortable, undisturbed nights in the adjoining room in April 1968, and the licensee, Mr Leslie Berridge, confesses that he has not seen the ghost himself. But several of his guests have. One regular visitor who often occupies the room has seen it several times, and 'he's a well-balanced sort of chap who doesn't drink much', says Mr Berridge.

The King's Head at Altarnun in Cornwall, a sixteenth-century coaching inn, is occasionally visited by the ghost of a former occupant named Peggy Bray. Another haunted Cornish pub is the famous Jamaica Inn. The story is that many years ago a man who was drinking there was told he was wanted outside. As soon as he stepped out of the door he was attacked and killed. Since then he has been seen periodically sitting on a wall outside the inn, but he neither moves nor speaks.

Juliet, who is supposed to haunt the Ferry Boat Inn by the River Ouse at Holywell in Huntingdonshire on 17 March each year, has never been seen by anybody. Juliet was a love-lorn girl who hanged herself from a willow near the river and was buried in unhallowed ground nearby, under an unmarked slab of stone. Years later the inn was built round the grave, the stone forming part of the floor, and the tradition grew that Juliet emerged from under the stone on the anniversary of her death. As at Guisborough Priory, hopeful crowds tend to visit the Ferry Boat on the evening the ghost should appear; but Juliet remains strangely shy. Yet odd things undoubtedly have happened at the inn and there are local people who deliberately keep away from the place on 17 March.

The numerous theatrical ghosts never, of course, fluff their entrances. Both Dan Leno and Charles Keen have been seen in the Theatre Royal, Drury Lane, since their deaths, but a better known spectre is the Man in Grey, a handsome young man in eighteenth-century costume, with sword and tricorne hat, who keeps most regular hours, haunting the theatre only between nine in the morning and six in the evening. He has been seen many times by actors, cleaners and members of the audience, but since his appearance invariably heralds a successful run, nobody wants him exorcised. It is thought likely that he is the ghost of a man whose skeleton was found bricked up in a small room over a century ago. But it is odd that the dagger found in the skeleton's ribs was of the Cromwellian period.

An equally active ghost is that of William Terriss, who was stabbed to death by a mad actor in Maiden Lane outside a back entrance to the Adelphi Theatre on 16 December 1897. One might expect him to haunt this spot, and indeed he has been seen there once and his footsteps heard several times. But his favourite haunting place is, strangely, Covent Garden Underground station, where he has been seen many times by station staff—always in November or December—at least as lately as 1964.

# CHAPTER
## TEN

# GHOSTS ON THE ROAD

IT is not only buildings that are haunted. Roads too have their ghosts. In fact one sometimes gets the impression that if all the phantom coaches driven by headless coachmen were taken off the highways it would relieve a great deal of congestion. The most famous of these ghostly coaches is probably that which carries Anne Boleyn to Blickling Hall in Norfolk on the anniversary of her execution, which took place on 19 May 1536. Blickling, along with Rochford Hall in Essex which she also reputedly haunts, is claimed as her birthplace. Hever Castle, her father's home in Kent where the young King Henry spent many happy days, is also traditionally associated with her. She spent much of her childhood at Blickling, and was greatly attached to the house, which explains her annual visit there.

Wearing a white dress and holding her detached head in her hands, she arrives just before midnight in a black coach drawn by four headless horses controlled by a headless coachman. The coach drives up the avenue to the front door of this lovely mansion—rebuilt shortly after her time—and disappears at the hall door. But Anne's ghost glides through the corridors of the house. W. A. Dutt said that many people had seen the phantom coach and the ghost of Anne.

Anne's father, Sir Thomas Bullen, also has a phantom coach drawn by headless horses. In this, and accompanied by a pack of fiends uttering spine-chilling cries, he has to cross forty county bridges in Norfolk in a single night as an act of penance for some unspecified crime.

An even more alarming Norfolk coach that Dutt seems to

have missed is a four-in-hand that drives from the village of
Bastwick at midnight on 31 May each year. It is driven by a
mad coachman, throws out sparks from its wheels and appears
to be on fire, though this does not trouble its occupants, who
are skeletons anyway. Eventually this coach strikes the stonework of Potter Heigham Bridge, is smashed to pieces and its
driver, horses, and occupants thrown into the water. According to Charles Sampson, who says that it was seen in 1926 and
1930, it commemorates the marriage of Sir Godfrey Haslitt of
Bastwick Place, and Evelyn, Lady Montefiore Carew of Castle
Lynn; a marriage into which he was trapped by the bride's
scheming mother, who sold her soul to the devil to achieve
her aim. After the marriage in Norwich Cathedral on 31 May
1741, the devil claimed his own, with disastrous results to all
concerned. Bastwick Place was burnt down on the same night.

Devon roads, especially those around Dartmoor, are also
better avoided at night. On the Okehampton–Tavistock road,
for instance, you are liable any night to meet the notorious
Lady Howard riding in a coach of bones, drawn by headless
horses with a headless coachman in charge, as usual. There
are many variations of the Lady Howard story. She lived in
the seventeenth century at Fitzford House, Tavistock, among
other places, and seems to have been an unpleasant character
who survived—and possibly murdered—four husbands. By
way of reparation, she has to drive every midnight from
Tavistock to Okehampton Castle to collect one blade of grass
to lay in the courtyard at Fitzford House, and to go on doing
this until every blade has been moved. The blade is carried
in the mouth of a black hound that trots alongside the
carriage. Another version has it that her mission has nothing
to do with grass but is to fetch the souls of the dying from
around Okehampton.

In the same area you may possibly encounter the ghost of
Sir Francis Drake, of all unlikely people, riding in a black
coach drawn by the inevitable headless horses. Behind his

coach runs a pack of hounds whose baying is fatal to any dog hearing it.

The Westcountry and Wales have many phantom coach stories. A ghostly coach has been seen many times near Coombe in Wiltshire, and another frequents the Salisbury–Hungerford road. But this part of Britain has no monopoly in phantom coaches. Edinburgh has one that drives up the Lawnmarket on certain nights in the year driven by six ghostly horses. Beverley has one hauled by four headless horses. It is driven by the headless ghost of Sir Jocelyn Percy, who is apparently expiating an act of sacrilege.

At midnight on Christmas Eve one is supposed to hear the screaming of horses coming from Black Greve Farm, Wythall, just south of Birmingham. These screams have echoed down the ages from about AD 47 when a Roman chariot, hauled by a pair of horses, careered off the snow-covered, hedgeless road and plunged into the moat at Black Greve. Another version says it was a carriage and four of much later date, and in this form it is similar to stories from Trent in Dorset and Great Melton in Norfolk, except that in these latter stories the screams are not confined to Christmas Eve, and the Great Melton coach contained a bridal party.

Phantom funeral processions are not unknown. One is sometimes seen in Lyme Park, Cheshire, the coach followed by a mourning woman in white. The story is that this is the funeral procession of Sir Piers Legh, whose family lived at Lyme Hall for centuries. Sir Piers died of wounds in France in 1422 and was brought back to his native Cheshire for burial. The woman is not his widow but his mistress, who died of a broken heart when told of his death. At Marnhull in Dorset a funeral procession has been seen at midnight not far from a quarry where many human remains were found in 1870, and a headless funeral procession has been seen in the same county near Milborne St Andrew. The Long Mynd in Shropshire has another ghostly funeral procession which is

sometimes seen at dusk moving towards Ratlinghope at a
goodish pace. Its origin is unknown, but the Long Mynd at
twilight is just the sort of wild high plateau where one would
expect to see ghostly visitations.

The roads of the Derbyshire High Peak have a similarly
eerie quality, and it was on the road leading from Bamford
to the Snake Pass that Mr John J. Grover of Rotherham had
a baffling experience. He was riding his motor-cycle towards
the junction with the Snake when he saw in the light of his
headlamp that he was overtaking a horse and cart. The cart
was of unusual design, with high sides and back. The driver,
wearing a long coat and tall hat, was walking alongside the
horse and holding a long whip. Mr Grover was about to
overtake when he saw the lights of a car approaching, so he
pulled in behind the cart and dimmed his own headlight.
The motorist, less considerate, kept his headlight undimmed,
momentarily dazzling Mr Grover. On recovering, he pulled
out to pass the cart, but found to his astonishment that the
road was empty.

'Thinking that perhaps the horse had taken fright and
gone into the ditch,' wrote Mr Grover, 'I got off my bicycle
and searched the side of the road, which there fell off rather
steeply.' But there was no sign of horse, cart or driver, and no
turnings off the road for nearly half a mile. There is no
explanation and no sequel; no tradition that the road is
haunted. But Mr Grover was convinced that he had imagined
nothing.

Phantom horsemen, some of them headless, haunt many
roads. One near Skipsea in Yorkshire is not only headless but
rides a headless horse. Another lane, leading from the Pil-
grim's Way to Bearsted in Kent, is haunted by a ghostly
horseman who wears a broad-brimmed hat and silver spurs
and sometimes appears in daylight, but never leaves any trace
of a hoofmark. My favourite phantom horseman is the ghost
of Simon Cunliffe, squire of Wycoller Hall in Lancashire,

who still rides the moorland around his old home and sounds his hunting-horn when a tragedy is imminent. His story is that he was out hunting one day when the fox tried to take refuge in the hall itself, where it bolted up the stairs. Cunliffe, in hot pursuit, rode up the staircase of his own home and into his wife's room, giving her a fatal shock. Until quite recently, hoofmarks could still be seen on two steps of the staircase, but the hall is now a ruin and I am told that the staircase has been removed.

Not all ghosts of the roads belong to the days of coaches and horsemen. Phantom motor vehicles have begun to appear in recent years. A motor car is sometimes seen to cross the Swindon–Huntingford road at a spot where there are barbed wire fences on either side. A phantom bus has been seen on the road between Lamberhurst and Frant on the Kent–Sussex border by most reliable witnesses who have on occasions stopped or even pulled into gateways to allow it room to pass —but it just has not passed.

The road between Postbridge and Two Bridges on Dartmoor was said by the press to be haunted after a series of accidents around 1921. An army officer claimed that a pair of hairy hands had seized his and pushed him and his motorcycle off the road. The road was examined by experts, the camber found to be faulty, and alterations were made. But strange accidents have continued to occur on this road, and Mrs Ruth E. St Leger-Gordon says that a woman sleeping in a caravan near the road about 1924 saw two large hairy hands crawling up the window.

Part of the main Sheffield–Manchester road between Hyde and Mottram in Cheshire acquired a similar reputation at one time. On one particular stretch of nearly straight road with a good surface there were sixteen major accidents over a period of twenty-two months in 1929–30, involving three deaths and twenty-five injuries. For none of these could any satisfactory explanation be given, according to the local coroner, who was so concerned that he took his jury at midnight to visit the scene of these accidents to see if any particular trick of light could account for the trouble.

The particular fatal accident that was being investigated was to a pillion passenger on his cousin's motor-cycle. The driver, who survived a fractured skull, attributed the accident to his having to swerve suddenly to avoid a motor-lorry which backed out from an opening by an inn. But the local police said that there was no opening there and no evidence of there having been a lorry in the vicinity.

The press investigated the story thoroughly and several local residents, including the licensee of the inn, came up with stories of strange footsteps heard around the houses just before the accidents occurred. The story faded out, but six months later there was a further spate of accidents in the same spot. The police put constant patrols on the road; a wall and fence that might have looked like the back of a lorry were removed, but the road is still believed by some people to be haunted. As is a stretch of the Penrith–Carlisle road where similar unaccountable accidents have occurred.

A road near Alconbury in Huntingdonshire is haunted by the ghost of a nun, whose sudden appearance has caused cars to brake hurriedly, and it may have been on that same road— it was certainly in that same district—that a married couple I know had an unnerving experience. Heading home for Derbyshire one night, they rounded a bend to find three cars in a ditch with three men standing by surveying the wreckage. My friends pulled up, and the husband went back to see if he could help. To his surprise, none of the men took the slightest notice of him. Eventually, rather nettled, he returned to his own car, noticing as he went that all the wrecked cars seemed to be pretty old models. He explained the position to his wife, and was about to drive off when he glanced in his mirror and saw all three cars and the three men enveloped in a sheet of flames.

H

As there seemed nothing he could do there, my friend drove off to the next village—he does not know its name, but I do not for a moment doubt his word—and reported the incident to the policeman, who just smiled and said, 'We often get this incident reported, sir'. But it was six months before my friend's wife would go out in the car again at night.

# CHAPTER ELEVEN

# HELL-HOUNDS AND OTHER PETS

EQUALLY as unpleasant as the phantom vehicles that one may meet on the roads of Britain are the strange beasts that roam at night in many parts of the country, often presaging death to those they meet.

One of the best known of these fearsome creatures is Black Shuck, more affectionately called 'Old Shuck' by the local populace, who haunts the north Norfolk coast between Brancaster and Overstrand. He is a shaggy dog (*shuck* means shaggy in the local dialect) about the size of a cow, who howls abominably according to some people and remains silent according to others. Round Brancaster he is thought to bring death within a year to those who see him, but in the Overstrand area, where there is a Shuck Lane, his effects are less lethal. Whether he has two eyes and fire dripping from his jaw, as some say, or no head but one blazing eye, as others believe, he would be a startling monster to meet on those highly atmospheric salt-marshes that separate Salthouse, Cley and Blakeney from the sea. Sheringham people say he is a dog washed ashore at Beeston from a shipwreck, but F. R. Buckley thinks this is a rationalisation of a race-memory and has advanced the theory that 'Old Shuck' is Fenris, the Wolf of Hell, who in Norse mythology symbolises the death that springs from sin.

Uplyme, the first village in Devon when you climb the steep hill out of Lyme Regis, also has a black dog haunting its lanes, particularly those close to The Black Dog Hotel, which takes its name from this creature. The Uplyme black dog is less dangerous than most in that its appearance does

not necessarily herald death. In fact it was originally guardian of treasure hidden in a local farmhouse. For years,
according to J. R. W. Coxhead, it haunted this farmhouse
without causing much concern to the farmer, who had grown
quite fond of it. However, one night, in a fit of irritation, he
struck at it with a poker, whereupon the dog rushed round
the house and then escaped by tearing a hole in the thatched
roof. When the subsequent repairs were being carried out, a
large sum of money was found at the foot of the rafters.

Much less friendly are Padfoot, the Yorkshire ghost-dog,
or the similar shaggy black dog that infests the Burnley district of Lancashire. Both bring death to those who see them,
while Swaledale's headless black dog also foretells some tragic
event. The black dog that appears only to the Vaughans of
Shropshire is a sign of a forthcoming death in the family.

Barguest is a creature common to both northern and southern England. He usually appears in the form of a hound, but
can apparently turn himself at will into some other form of
animal. He always indicates approaching death or disaster. It
was some such creature as this that gave Sir Arthur Conan
Doyle the idea for his *Hound of the Baskervilles*.

These monsters are not an exclusively British phenomenon; similar hell-hounds abound in northern Europe and
are probably linked with the 'wild hunt' stories that may date
back to the days of the pagan nature gods. These wild hunts-
men and their packs of ghostly hounds ride out at certain
times—perhaps when the nation is in danger—or on certain
nights of the year, or sometimes just at random. The most
famous of them is Hearne the Hunter, who tears through
Windsor Great Park with his spectral hounds. Two very
frightened Eton boys said they saw them when returning to
college through the park towards the end of the last century.

Wild Edric and his men who haunt the Shropshire lead-
mining country in times of national danger apparently have
no hounds, but Dartmoor has Dewer and his Wish (or Wisk)

Hounds, who race to destruction over the edge of Dewer Stone at the southern tip of the moor, bringing death within a year to any who see them.

Charming Purse Caundle Manor in Dorset is visited by King John's hounds on Midsummer's Eve and either Christmas Eve or New Year's Eve, depending on which version you accept. The hounds and horns are only heard—nobody has seen the hunt—but the housekeeper and cook are said to have heard them as recently as 1959. The present house is Tudor, but an earlier mansion on the site was known as King John's House, because that unpopular monarch used it as a hunting lodge.

A hound that troubles nobody is Gelert, whose grave at Beddgelert is an essential place of pilgrimage to visitors to North Wales. There are numerous versions of the Gelert story the world over, but the one most commonly accepted in Wales is that he was given by King John to his son-in-law Prince Llywellyn in 1205 and became the favourite hound of this sporting prince. One day, however, he vanished from the pack during a hunt which proved abortive. Llywellyn returned home disgruntled to find the hound covered with blood standing by the overturned cradle of the prince's young child. Llywellyn, jumping to conclusions, immediately drew his sword and killed the hound, which he thought had slaughtered his child. Too late, he discovered the child safe under the cradle with a dead wolf lying nearby.

Nearly 600 years later, the then landlord of the Royal Goat Hotel at Beddgelert put up a stone on a spot called the Dog's Grave, according to Mr D. Parry-Jones, and did his hotel a great deal of good financially. The ghost of this landlord, David Pritchard, is said to haunt the hotel, perhaps merely to gloat over the results of his flair for publicity, as he seems a harmless, cheerful ghost as ghosts go.

Perhaps the best known of all animal legends is the story of the monster Dun Cow who, having been bewitched, escaped from Mitchell's Fold, a stone circle on an outlier of Corndon Hill in west Shropshire, to make a nuisance of herself to everybody in the Warwickshire countryside. She was eventually slain by the legendary Guy of Warwick, whose name is perpetuated by the house called Guy's Cliffe, now in ruins just outside Warwick, just as the name of the Dun Cow is perpetuated by an inn at Dunchurch.

The Dun Cow story has a sequel. The animal is said to reappear before the death of a member of the Earl of Warwick's family. A visitor to Warwick Castle late in the nineteenth century, knowing nothing of the story, saw a dun-coloured cow trampling over a lawn there one evening, but could find no trace of hoof marks next morning. On reporting her story to Lady Warwick, she was promptly silenced. A few days later the earl died.

The death of a Bishop of Chichester is said to be imminent when a heron sits on the pinnacle of the cathedral spire. Defoe tells of a butcher 'standing at his shop-door in the South Street' who saw a heron on the spire and 'ran in for his gun, and being a good marksman shot the heron, and kill'd it, at which his mother was very angry with him, and said he had kill'd the bishop, and the next day news came to the town that Dr Williams, the last bishop, was dead; this is affirm'd by many people, inhabitants of the place.' The appearance of two large birds on the roof of Salisbury Cathedral is said to forecast the death of the Bishop of Salisbury.

The Oxenham family of Oxenham Manor in Devon are said to be haunted by a white bird which appears before the death of one of the family. This bird does not confine its appearance to the manor itself—once the home of that John Oxenham who sailed with Drake—but is liable to appear wherever the family is staying.

Northumberland, Durham and North Yorkshire seem to have been seriously troubled by 'worms' in ancient times, for there are numerous stories from the north-east dealing with the activities of these strange, unpleasant-sounding creatures, of which the Lambton and Loftus Worms are the most celebrated. They may have been mere snakes that time has magnified, but Peter A. White has advanced the theory that Durham was 'the last breeding ground of prehistoric leftovers', and it does seem possible that the worm legends are founded on folk-memories of ancient creatures that once infested north country bogs.

The Lambton Worm, fairly typical of its genre, caused as much trouble in County Durham as the Dun Cow in Warwickshire, satisfying its hunger by swallowing children and its thirst by milking a dozen cows or so at a time. Sir John Lambton, returning to Lambton Castle from fighting overseas, decided to put a stop to these excesses. Having consulted local witches and soothsayers, he accepted the advice that the most suitable place to fight the worm would be in the River Wear, whose current would sweep away pieces of the creature before they could re-form. In payment for this advice he had to offer the life of the first living creature to emerge from the castle after the fight. The rest of the story is reminiscent of the Devil's Bridge legends in reverse. Sir John arranged that his father would send out a dog after the worm had been killed, but when the worm had been successfully disposed of—with some difficulty—Lord Lambton, in his excitement, dashed out of the castle to congratulate his son. Quickly realising his mistake, he turned back for the dog, but he was too late, and it is said that the next fourteen generations of Lambtons died violently.

If all the worms are now extinct, there are still adders on the banks of the River Derwent, a tributary of the Tyne. They are especially prolific where the river forms the boundary of the Derwentwater estate. And the odd thing is that there were none along the river at all before 1715. Indeed they appeared for the first time on the day that Lord Derwentwater, a popular local figure, was executed for his part

Page 133 (above) *Lyme Hall, Cheshire, is double haunted;* (below) *the ghost of Anne Boleyn is said to pass through this entrance to Blickling Hall, Norfolk, on each anniversary of her execution*

Page 134 (above) *The haunted road into Ratlinghope from the Long Mynd, Salop;* (below) *King John's hounds visit Purse Caundle Manor, Dorset, twice a year*

Page 135 (above) *The Dun Cow Hotel, Dunchurch, Warwickshire, named after a local monster;* (below) *Warwick Castle features in the Dun Cow story*

GODIVA

THEN SHE RODE BACK CLOTHED ON WITH
CHASTITY SHE TOOK THE TAX AWAY AND
BUILT HERSELF AN EVERLASTING NAME

Page 136
(left) *Lady Godiva's statue at Coventry, Warwickshire;* (below) *Exton Old Hall, Rutland, possible setting of the Mistletoe Bough legend*

in the Old Pretender's rising of that year.

Perhaps the local inhabitants should try the bell remedy that has wiped out the adders that used to infest the banks of the Thames at Dorchester-on-Thames in Oxfordshire. Legend has it that St Berin, a Wessex saint, died there from an adder bite in 650, but when a tenor bell was placed in the abbey tower in his memory all the adders vanished. The present tenor bell, cast about 1380, has a Latin inscription calling on St Berin's protection, but adders are not specially mentioned.

The land around Whitby Abbey was also reputed to be infested with snakes until St Hilda went there as prioress. After praying that they might all be thrown into the sea, she drove them to the edge of the cliff and broke off their heads with a whip. They fell over the edge with their bodies curled up. Later they turned into stone and are still to be found at the foot of the cliffs round Whitby, though geologists dismiss them as ammonites.

# CHAPTER
# TWELVE

# ODDS AND ENDS

T HERE are various British legends that fit into no particular category, but can hardly be left out of a book of this nature. One is the mistletoe bough story, so named because of a popular music hall song of 1828 called 'The Mistletoe Bough', based on an earlier ballad. It began:

> The mistletoe hung in the castle hall
> The holly branch hung on the old oak wall

As usual, there are several differing versions, but the basic outline of the tale is of a girl who during Christmas festivities in some country mansion hid herself in an oak chest in an obscure attic while taking part in a game of hide-and-seek. Some accounts heighten the pathos by adding that it was her wedding night and that she hoped to be found by her bridegroom. Unfortunately, she could not be found at all, nor could she open the chest lid. After a lengthy search her body was discovered, but by then she had died of suffocation.

The story may well be based on fact, but if so where did it happen? The ruined manor house at Minster Lovell, now a Department of the Environment property, on the banks of the Windrush, is a hot favourite. They say there that the victim was Lord Lovell's bride and that her skeleton, still wearing a wedding dress, was not discovered for fifty years. But the Minster Lovell legend is probably an embroidered version of a very similar tragedy that really did take place there. In 1487, five years after the house was built, the then Lord Lovell was on the losing side in the Battle of Stoke

during the rebellion against Henry VII. He escaped to his
Oxfordshire home and hid in a secret room which he had
prepared as a hide-out. The pursuing soldiers failed to locate
the secret room, which could be opened only from the outside
by a secret spring, a fact known solely by one trusted servant.
Unfortunately, the servant, alarmed by the soldiers, died
suddenly of a heart attack, leaving the luckless Lord Lovell
to die slowly of starvation. In fact his body was not discovered
until a new chimney was put in in 1708. It seems too much
of a coincidence that there should have been two such similar tragedies in one house.

So if not Minster Lovell, where? The lovely Stuart mansion at Bramshill in Hampshire is reputedly haunted by a
bride in her wedding dress, and the tragic oak chest was still
on view there in the early nineteenth century, but Brian
Vesey-Fitzgerald, who knows Hampshire inside-out, thinks
that Marwell has a much stronger claim. Up in the Midlands
they settle for Exton, where the old and new (new only by
comparison) manor houses stand side by side in one of the
most delightful villages in the lovely but comparatively
unknown county of Rutland. And there are other houses
around the country that put forward equally strong claims
to have been the scene of this tragedy.

A rather similar situation used to apply to the birthplace
of that famous pantomime hero, Dick Whittington. He was
a real person who married his boss's daughter and became
Lord Mayor of London three times between 1389 and 1419,
before being knighted in 1423. The story of his turning at
the sound of Bow Bells could also be true, but the cat is
almost certainly a later twist to the story. There now seems
little doubt that he was a Gloucestershire man, born in 1359,
almost certainly at Pauntley. A commemorative plaque now
hangs on the wall of Pauntley Court, former home of the
Whittington family.

Two other pantomime characters, the Babes in the Wood,

are supposed to haunt Wayland Wood, near Watton in Nor-folk. They were reputedly orphans left in the care of a 'wicked uncle' who hired two ruffians to murder them. The men lost their nerve finally, leaving the children to wander in the wood, where they eventually starved to death. The uncle came to a sticky end after a series of misfortunes. The wailing of the babes can still be heard in the wood on stormy nights, or so Dutt said.

Coventry, of course, has undisputed claim to Lady Godiva, wife of Earl Leofric, ruler of the Midland province of Mercia. Recent research has established that she died in September 1067, but there is no proof that she rode naked through the streets of Coventry, though one has to be pretty brave to cast doubts on it in that flourishing Midland city. The traditional tale is that Godiva pleaded with her husband to ease the heavy burden of taxation that he had placed on the Coventry people. He replied, 'I will reduce the taxes if you ride naked through the town'. She accepted the challenge and rode out one dawn, 'her only mantle the long golden hair which cascaded down to conceal part of her lovely form'. The streets were empty as the townspeople had agreed to remain indoors behind barred shutters during her ride. Only an apprentice tailor named Tom broke the pact by peeping through the shutters as Godiva passed, and was immediately struck blind.

Peeping Tom may have been a purely legendary charac-ter. There are even people who dare to suggest that the ride itself is a legend based on fertility rites. A second theory is that it was only the horse that was naked, without bridle or saddle. Miss Joan Lancaster, a former archivist of Coventry, and her collaborator Dr Hilda Davidson, suggest that 'she may have ridden in beggar's garb ... but she would hardly ride around naked in the eleventh century', but none of these theories cut much ice in Coventry, where a statue by Sir William Reid Dick was erected in the city centre in 1949 to commemorate the ride.

The villagers of Gotham, near Nottingham, are less enthusiastic about their reputation for being the most foolish
people in Britain, though they tend to shrug off the stories
with a certain wry pride. It was their ancestors, we are told,
who built a high hedge to pen in a cuckoo in order to enjoy
her song all the year round, and then cursed themselves for
not building it higher when the bird flew away. These same
people pulled down one of their two windmills to allow the
other to catch all the wind, attempted to drown an eel in a
pond and burned down a forge to smoke out a wasp's nest.
These stories go back over 400 years, and in 1662 Dr Fuller
wrote that 'a hundred fopperies are reigned and fathered on
the town folk of Gotham'.

Gotham still has its Cuckoo Bush Hill and Cuckoo Bush
Inn to recall its foolish past, but it has no exclusive rights to
the hedge story. Borrowdale, Madeley in Shropshire, and
Austwick in Yorkshire have similar traditions. Indeed most
counties, one suspects, have their villages of which such
stories are told.

There is only one village in Britain, so far as I know, that
is, or has been, completely haunted. This is Great Leigh in
Essex. The troubles began in 1944 when some United States
Air Force men from a nearby aerodrome moved a stone that
was reputed to mark a witch's grave. From then on the oddest
things happened. Hens failed to lay, cows stopped giving
milk, animals strayed from fields which seemed secure, ricks
overturned and the church bell rang without human aid.
When the stone was eventually replaced, the hauntings
stopped, or almost stopped; the licensee of the St Anne's
Castle inn in the village maintains, however, that a ghost is
still active on his premises from time to time.

It is an odd story, but then Britain is full of odd, un-
explained happenings. Mr Francis Fisher, a scholarly local
historian, tells a story that he heard from an old lady of
an experience that befell her as a girl at the turn of the

century. She was playing with a friend in the school yard at Alvaston, a village now swallowed up by the borough of Derby, when they heard the sound of galloping horses, shouts and a pistol shot, which so unnerved them that they ran to the far end of the yard. They heard horses' hooves go by, followed quickly by another party of horsemen, both heading along a lane leading to Elvaston Castle. But they saw nothing. Nor did they know then that there had been a skirmish at Elvaston between Roundheads and Cavaliers in the Civil War after a pursuit that must have followed that very lane.

So we have turned full circle and are back with phantom armies, of which there are many strange stories, and back again near the heart of this country of legends and ghosts.

# SOURCES AND FURTHER READING

ASHE, GEOFFREY. *King Arthur's Avalon* (Collins 1957). *From Caesar to Arthur* (Collins 1960). *The Quest for Arthur's Britain* (Pall Mall 1968)

BARDENS, D. *Ghosts and Hauntings* (Zeus Press 1965)

BENFIELD, E. *Dorset* (Hale 1950)

BENWELL, G. and WAUGH, A. *Sea Enchantress* (Hutchinson 1961)

BETTS, H. *English Myths and Traditions* (Batsford 1952)

BIRLEY, SIR ROBERT. *The Underground of History* (Historical Association 1955)

BRADDOCK, JOSEPH. *Haunted Houses* (Batsford 1956)

BURNE, C. S. *Folk-Lore, Legends and Old Customs in Memorials of Old Shropshire* (Bemrose & Sons 1906)

COXHEAD, J. R. W. *Devon Traditions and Fairy Tales* (Raleigh Press 1959)

CRAWFORD, O. G. S. 'Arthur and his Battles', *Antiquity* (Sept 1935)

CROUCH, M. *Kent*, 2nd edition (Batsford 1967)

DACOMBE, M. R. (ed). *Dorset Up Along and Down Along* (Dorset Women's Institute 1935)

DAY, J. WENTWORTH. 'The Ghosts of Athelhampton', *Country Life* (1 Dec 1966)

J

DE SELINCOURT, A. *The Channel Shore* (Hale 1963)

DUTT, W. A. *Highways and Byways in East Anglia* (Macmillan 1932)

FINDLER, G. *Legends of the Lake Counties* (Dalesman 1967)

FIRTH, J. B. *Highways and Byways in Nottinghamshire* (Macmillan 1916)

FLETCHER, H. L. V. *Herefordshire* (Hale 1948)

GEE, H. L. *Folk-Tales of Yorkshire* (Nelson 1952)

GRICE, F. L. *Folk-Tales of the West Midlands* (Nelson 1952). *Lord Halifax's Ghost Book* (Fontana 1967)

GROVER, JOHN J. Letter to *Country Life* (25 Jan 1952)

HALIFAX, LORD. *see* Grice, F. L.

HARRIS, P. V. *The Truth about Robin Hood*, 3rd edition (published by the author in 1954)

HAWKINS, D. *Sedgemoor and Avalon* (Hale 1954)

HOLE, C. *Haunted England*, 2nd edition (Batsford 1950). *Saints in Folklore* (Bell 1966)

HOLT, J. C. 'The Ballades of Robin Hood', *Past and Present* (18 Nov 1960)

HUSSEY, CHRISTOPHER. 'Littlecote, Wilts', *Country Life* (25 Nov, 2, 9 and 16 Dec 1965)

KEEN, M. *Outlaws of Medieval Legend* (Routledge 1961)

LANCASTER, JOAN, and DAVIDSON, HILDA. *Godiva of Coventry* (Coventry Corporation 1967)

LEES-MILNE, J. *Historic Houses, Castles and Gardens in Great Britain* (Index 1968)

LESLIE, SIR S. *Ghost Book* (Hollis & Carter 1955)

LOOMIS, R. S. *The Development of the Arthurian Romance* (Hutchinson 1963)

LUDLAM, H. *The Restless Ghosts of Layde Place and other True Hauntings* (Foulsham 1967)

MACGREGOR, A. A. *Phantom Footsteps* (Hale 1959)

MACPHERSON, CAPTAIN HARVEY. *The Field* (7 Sept 1967)

MASSINGHAM, H. J. *The Southern Marches* (Hale 1952)

NORTH, F. J. *Sunken Cities* (University of Wales 1957)

O'DONNELL, E. *Ghosts with a Purpose* (Rider 1952) compiled by H. Ludlam. *The Midnight Hearse and More Ghosts* (Foulsham 1965)

PARKIN, MICHAEL. 'The Ghost who wears Gumboots', *The Guardian* (31 Jan 1968)

PARRY-JONES, D. *Welsh Legends and Fairy Lore* (Batsford 1953)

RADFORD, E. and M. A. (revised by Christina Hole). *Encyclopaedia of Superstitions*, 2nd edition (Hutchinson 1961)

RIDLEY, N. *Portrait of Northumberland* (Hale 1965)

ROBINS, F. W. *The Smith* (Rider 1953)

RYDER, T. A. *Portrait of Gloucestershire* (Hale 1966)

ST LEGER-GORDON, R. E. *The Witchcraft and Folklore of Dartmoor* (Hale 1965)

SAKLATVALA, B. *Arthur: Roman Britain's Last Champion* (David & Charles 1967)

SAMPSON, C. *Ghosts of the Broads* (Yachtsman 1931)

SCOTT, H. J. *Portrait of Yorkshire* (Hale 1965)

SMITH, V. *Portrait of Dartmoor* (Hale 1966)

SPENCE, LEWIS. *Minor Traditions of British Mythology* (Rider 1948)

SPENCER, LEWIS. *The Outlines of Mythology* (Watts 1944)

STIRLING, A. M. W. *Ghosts Vivisected* (Hale 1957)

SWIFT, E. *Folk Tales of the East Midlands* (Nelson 1954)

THORPE, L. (trans and ed). *Geoffrey of Monmouth: The History of the Kings of Britain* (Penguin 1966)

TOWNSHEND OF RAYMOND, THE MARCHIONESS, and FFOULKES, M. C. *True Ghost Stories* (Hutchinson 1936)

TREHARNE, R. F. *The Glastonbury Legends* (Cresset 1967)

TURNER, M. LOVETT. *Somerset* (Hale 1949)

VESEY-FITZGERALD, B. *Hampshire and the Isle of Wight* (Hale 1949)

WALKER, J. W. *The True Story of Robin Hood* (published by the author in 1952)

WARREN, C. H. *Essex* (Hale 1950)

WHITE, P. A. *Portrait of County Durham* (Hale 1967)

WILLIAMS, GUY. *Enjoy Painting in Oils* (Gollancz 1963)

# ACKNOWLEDGEMENTS

MY debt to some of those who have already written on legends and ghosts is acknowledged either in the text or in the bibliography at the end of the book, and I have also found much useful material in such magazines as British Tourist Authority's *In Britain*, and those excellent county magazines that have so bravely avoided the temptation of becoming mere local echoes of the old *Tatler*.

Many of those who have helped me verbally I cannot thank because I do not even know their names; others are acknowledged in the text. I am deeply indebted to numerous county and borough librarians who, as always, have gone to great trouble to answer my queries, and I hope none will take it amiss if I offer special words of thanks to my old friend Mr Kenneth Smith, FLA, Borough Librarian of Carlisle, and to the invariably helpful staff at the Derby Borough Library. Another old friend, Mr Eric Fowler, MBE, has been particularly helpful in various ways, and I am equally grateful to the late Mr J. F. E. Merewether, Messrs S. J. Price, T. R. Sobey, News Editor of *Sussex Life*, Ernest Touchotte, Cyril Sprenger, and Nicholas R. Webber, staff reporter of the *Alton Herald*, among others. I am only sorry that so many of the stories that I have been given have had to be omitted for lack of space.

Finally, I must record my deep gratitude to my friend Mr Frank Rodgers for so kindly and ably taking so many photographs specifically for this book, and to my wife and daughter for their forbearance of my preoccupation with legends and ghosts.

# INDEX

❦

*References to illustrations are in italics.*

Aberystwyth, 20
Adders, 132, 137
Adlestrop, 56
Albury, 73
Alcock, Leslie, 25
Alconbury, 125–6
Aldborough, 48
Aldworth, 56
Allen, river, 66
Altarnun, 116
Alton, 115
Alvaston, 144
Aqualate Mere, 67
Arviragus, King, 19, 20
Ashe, Geoffrey, 19, 22, 26
Astley Castle, 96, *107*
Athelhampton Manor, 105–6
Austwick, 143
Avalon, 19, 21
Avon Gorge, 56
Aydon, 59

Babes in the Wood, 141–2
Badbury Rings, 26
Bala, 65
Bamburgh Castle, 26
Bambury Stone, 56
Barguest, 129
Barlborough Hall, 32
Barnsdale Forest, 33–4
Barnsley, 32
Bastwick, 121
Battle Abbey, 91
Beaulieu, 91, *107*
Beddgelert, 130
Bedevere, Sir, 23

Beeby, 86, *90*
Beggar's Bridge, 70
Bellister Castle, 99
Belstone, 57
Berkeley Castle, 63
Berridge, Leslie, 115–16
Berry Pomeroy Castle, 97
Bettiscombe Manor House, 111
Beverley, 122
Bewdley, 48
Bexley, 97
Bidford-on-Avon, 10
Birchover, 33–4
Birdoswald, 26
Birdsmoor Gate, 45
Birley, Sir Robert, 11
Birtsmorton Court, 58
Bisham Abbey, 99–100
Black Shuck, 128
Blaise Castle Woods, 56
Blakemere, 67–8
Blakey Topping, 48
Blenkinsopp Castle, 98
Blickling Hall, 120, *133*
Blidworth, 34
Blowing Stone, 57
Blythburgh, 44
Bodmin Moor, 26, 47
Boleyn, Anne, 88, 120, *133*
Bomere Pool, 66
Borrow, George, 65
Borrowdale, 143
Bosham, 11, 64
Boswell, James, 10
Boudon Hill, 25
Bourne, 37

Bramshill, 141
Brandon, 37
Bredon Hill, 56, 57
Brent Tor, 88
Brierley, Walter, 113
Brinsop, 58
Brooke, Rupert, 112
Brookland, 43, 53
Buckland Abbey, 97
Buckley, F. R., 113
Burnley, 84, 129
Burton Agnes, 110–11
Bury Lane, 39
Bury St Edmunds, 77
Buxton, 37
Bywell, 88

Cadbury Castle, 16, 24
Caerleon-on-Usk, 18, 22, 25, 27
Calvert, Ralph, 46
Cam, river, 24
Cambridge, 38
Camelford, 25, 26
Camelon, 25
Camelot, 16, 19, 24–6, 62
Canute, 11
Carlisle, 25
Carmarthen, 23
Cathlaw, 25
Chagford, 57
Chalgrove Field, 12
Chapman, John, 87–8, 90
Charlcote, 10
Chesterfield, 43, 53
Chichester, 131
Christchurch Priory, 85
Cirencester, 22
Codnor Castle, 102
Colwall Stone, 57
Combe Sydenham Hall, 60
Coombe, 122
Countless Stones, 55
Coventry, 136, 142
Craig-y-Dinas, 27
Crawford, O. G. S., 26

Cricker Creeping Stone, 57
Cromer, 64
Crosby Garrett, 85
Cross Mere, 66
Crowza Stones, 76
Culbone, 86
Cunliffe, Simon, 123–4
Cypher Linn, 66

Dale Abbey, 31
Darrel, Will, 102–3
Dart, river, 69
Dartmoor, 57, 121, 129–30
Deadman's Plack, 77
Derby, 42, 115
Derwentwater, Lord, 132, 137
Devil, the, 42–9, 53
Dewer, 129–30
Dorchester-on-Thames, 137
Dorstone, 26
Dozmary Pool, 26
Dragon Hill, 58
Drake, Sir Francis, 11, 59–60,
  121–2
Drake Stone, 57
Dun Cow, Dunchurch, 130–1, 135
Dunwich, 63

East Bergholt, 43–4
Edgar, King, 78
Edge Hill, 9–10
Edinburgh, 122
Edward, 78
Edwinstowe, 30–1
Eildon Hills, 27
Elfrida, 78–9
Elvaston, 144
Ercall Hill, 48
Ethelbert, King, 79
Ethelwold, 77–8
Excalibur, 26
Exton Old Hall, 136, 141

Filey Brigg, 47
Forde House, Newton Abbot, 97

Fountain Dale, 34
Fountains Abbey, 32, 34, 46
Friar Tuck, 34

Gelert, 130
Geoffrey of Monmouth, 21, 22, 23
Giraldus Cambrensis, 21, 66
Glamis, 94, 95
Glastonbury, 16–22, *17*, 45, 66
Godiva, Lady, 10, *136*, 142
Godney, 16
Goodrich Castle, 97–8
Goodwin Cup, 63
Goodwin Sands, 62–3
Gotham, 143
Grantchester, The Old Vicarage,
   112
Great Leigh, 143
Great Melton, 122
Grey Geese, the, 56
Grey Wethers, 57
Griffiths, Anne, 110–11
Grimsby, 11, 113
Guisborough Priory, 91, 116
Guy of Warwick, 10, 131

Haddon Hall, 12
Halter Devil Chapel, *36*, 42–3
Hampton Court Palace, 95
Harbottle Hill, 57
Harpham, 70–3
Hathersage, 32, 34
Haughton Castle, 99
Hauteville's Quoit, 56
Hawkins, Desmond, 19, 20–1
Heage, 113
Hell Kettles, 67
Hel Tor, 22
Hempstead, 38
Henry II, King, 21
Hereford, 79
Hereward the Wake, 37, 38
Hinckley, 88
Hoby, Lady Elizabeth, 99–100
Hole, Christina, 24

Hole of Horcum, 48
Holy Grail, 16, 20, 21
Holy Thorn, 16, *17*, 20, 21
Holywell (Flint), 80
Holywell (Huntingdonshire), 116
Horndon-on-the-Hill, 88
Houghton Hall, 104
Howard, Lady, 121
How Caple, 20
Howe Hill, 48
Hoxne, 77
Hull, 70
Hulland Ward, 42–3
Huntingdon, 38
Hurlers, the, 55
Hurstmonceaux Castle, 98
Hylton Castle, 98–9

Inns, *see under names of places*
Ippikin's Rock, 39
Isolde, 23

Jenny Greenteeth, 69
Jock's Leap, 59

Kelliwic, 26
Kenelm, 79
Kensington Palace, 97
Kilgrimod, 64
Kimbolton Castle, 96
King Arthur, 13, 16–27, *17*, *18*, 30,
   62
Kingsclere, 86–7
King's Lynn, 113
Kingston Lisle, 58
Kirkby Lonsdale, 46
Kirklees Priory, 32

Lambeth, 87
Lambton Worm, the, 131–2
Lamorna Cove, 68
Lanyon Quoit, *54*, 56
Leyland, 85
Liddington Camp, 26
Liskeard, 55

Littlecote, 102–3
Little John, 32
Little John's grave, *18*, 32
Little John's Well, 34
Little Salkeld, 56
Llandrillo-yn-Rhôs, 81
Llangorse Lake, 65–6
Llyn Llydaw, 27
Llys Helig, 64
Loftus Worm, 131–2
Long Compton, 52
Long Meg and her Daughters, 56
Long Mynd, The, 122–3, *134*
Longstone, 57
Loo Pool, 26
Loughton, 39
Loxley, 34
Ludlow, 34
Ludworth Moor, 33
Lyme Hall, 96–7, 122, *133*

Macpherson, Capt Harvey, 25
Madeley, 143
Madron, 57
Maes Knoll, 56
Major Oak, 30–1
Manners, John, 12
Marden, 79
Marnhull, 122
Marwell, 141
Mayfield, 45
Meare, 16
Meigle, 26
Melrose Abbey, 27
Men-an-Tol, 57
Merbach Hill, 26
Merlin, 23
Mermaids, 67–9
Mermaid's Pool, 67–8, *71*
Michelham Priory, 101–2
Milbourne St Andrew, 122
Minster Lovell, 140–1
Mirylees, Mrs, 20
Mistletoe Bough, *136*, 140–1
Mold, 12

Montgomery, 91
Moorends, 114
Mordred, 26
Motor vehicles, phantom, 124–6
Mount Badon, 25–6
Mugginton, *36*, 42

Nanteos, 20
Nennius, 22
Newark, 112
Newport (Salop), 67
Newton Abbot, 97
Newton-le-Willows, 114
Newstead Abbey, 100–1
Nottingham, 31, 37, 101, 114

Ockley, 115–16
Offerton Moor, 33
Okehampton, 121
Orford, 68–9
Otterford, 34
Oxenham Manor, 131

Padfoot, 129
Padstow, 68
Papplewick, 31
Parson and Clerk Rocks, 47
Paulsgrove, 19
Pauntley, 141
Pearce-Higgins, Canon J.D., 112
Peeping Tom, 10, 142
Peg O'Neil, 69
Peg Powler, 69
Pendour Cove, 68
Penmaenmawr, 55
Perth, 26
Plemonstall, 82
Pomparles Bridge, 26
Poole Harbour, 26
Poole's Cavern, 37
Porlock, 86
Portsmouth Harbour, 19
Potter Heigham Bridge, 121
Potter Thompson, 27
Purse Caundle Manor, 130, *134*

Queen Camel, 24
Quendryda, 79
Queniborough, 86

Radway, 10
Raggedstone Hill, 58
Ratlinghope, 122–3, *134*
Ravenspur, 63
Raynham Hall, 103–4
Richmond Castle, 27
Ripple, 44–5
Roads, haunted, 120–6
Robin Hood, 30–8, *35*
Robin Hood's Bay, 34, *35*
Rochester Castle, 98, *108*
Rollright Stones, 9, 52–5
Romsley, 80
Roslyn Chapel, 85–6
Rudston, 49

St Augustine's Well, Cerne
 Abbas, 81, *89*
St Bartholomew-the-Great,
 Smithfield, 88
St Bees Head, 82
St Berga, 82
St Beunno, 80
St Chad, 80–1
St Chad's Well, Stowe, 80–1, *89*
St Dunstan, 16, 45
St Edmund, 77
St Edward, 77
St Joseph of Arimathea, 16, 19,
 20, 21
St Just, 76
St Keverne, 76
St Michael, 76
St Michael's Mount, 22, 76
St Milburga, 81
St Osyth, 80
St Patrick, 16
St Paul, 16, 19
St Peter-ad-Vincula, 88
St Plegmund, 82
St Robert of Knaresborough, 82

St Swithun, 82
St Trillo's Well, 81, 82
St Wilfred, 63
St Winifrede, 80
St Winifrede's Well, 80
Saklatvala, Beram, 25
Salle, 88
Sandford Orcas Manor, 104–5
Sawston Hall, 96
Scarborough, 34, 48
Seaton Delavel Hall, 99
Sedgemoor, 19
Selsey, 63
Semer Water, 65
Sewingshields Crags, 27
Shaftesbury Abbey, 78
Shardlow, 114
Sherwood Forest, 30–4
Shobdon, 44
Silbury Hill, 48
Silchester, 22
Silent Pool, 73
Skipsea, 123
Slack, 25
Snake Pass, 123
Slaughter Bridge, 26
South Petherton Bridge, 70
Spey, river, 69
Stanage Edge, 33
Stanner Rocks, 47
Stanton Drew, 55, 56
Steetley, 31
Stilton, 39
Stiperstones Ridge, 47, *54*
Stocklinch, 88
Stoke St Milborough, 81
Stonehenge, 23
Stowe-Nine-Churches, 84
Sutton Montis, 24
Sutton Walls, 79
Swaffham, 87–8, 90
Swarkestone Bridge, 69–70, *71*
Swindon, 113
Sydenham, Elizabeth, 59–60
Symond's Yat, 27

Tavistock, 121
Tees, river, 69
Teignmouth, 47
Tenterden Church, 62
Thaxted, *35*, 38
Theatres, haunted, 116–17
Thorncombe, 45
Thorpe, 46
Thorsby Hall, 32
Thrybergh, 59
Tidenham, 59
Tintagel, *17*, 23
Trent (Dorset), 122
Trent, river, 69–70, *71*
Tristan, 23
Tunbridge Wells, 45
Tunstead, *108*, 111–12
Turpin, Dick, *35*, *38–9*
Tweed, river, 69

Uplyme, 128–9
Upsall, 88

Vernon, Dorothy, 12
Veryan, *36*, 47

Wakefield, 33–4
Wardley Hall, 111
Warwick, 10, 131, *135*

Wayland Smith's Cave, 57
Wayland Wood, 141–2
Welton, 38
Wenlock Edge, 39
Westwood Church, 85
Wherwell, 79
Whitby, 64, 72, 137
Whitcliffe Scar, 58
Whittington, Dick, 141
Whittle, 85
Widecombe, 44
Willance's Leap, 59
Willingale Doe, 88
Willingale, Spain, 88
Wimbish, 38
Winchcombe, 79
Winchester, 22, 23, 82
Windsor Castle, 95
Windsor Great Park, 129
Wintour's Leap, 59
Winwick, 84
Wrekin, 48
Wroughton-on-the-Green, 39
Wycoller Hall, 123–4
Wythall, 122

York, 38–9

Zennor, 56, 68